MW01613916

Take-Home Books

Grade 6

Learning Resource Center
University of Tennessee, Martin
School of Education
217 Gooch Hall
Martin, TN 38238-5029

Harcourt

Orlando   Boston   Dallas   Chicago   San Diego

Visit *The Learning Site!*
www.harcourtschool.com

Copyright © by Harcourt, Inc.

All rights reserved. No part of this publication may be reproduced or transmitted in any form or by any means, electronic or mechanical, including photocopy, recording, or any information storage and retrieval system.

Teachers using COLLECTIONS may photocopy complete pages in sufficient quantities for classroom use only and not for resale.

HARCOURT and the Harcourt Logo are trademarks of Harcourt, Inc.

Printed in the United States of America

ISBN 0-15-313366-X

1 2 3 4 5 6 7 8 9 10   054   2003 2002 2001 2000

Contents

Harcourt

TAKE-HOME BOOK
Times of Discovery
Use with "The Best School Year Ever."

The Balloon Popper

by Karen Stamfil
illustrated by Jesse Clay

Simple Machines

The six kinds of simple machines are: (1) inclined plane, (2) wheel and axle, (3) lever, (4) pulley, (5) screw, and (6) wedge. See how many of them you can identify in Matt and Delia's balloon popper. Then number a sheet of paper 1 to 6. List an example of each kind of simple machine in your home or school.

School-Home Connection Listen as your child reads the book aloud. Then, as a family activity, design a machine like the one in the story, but give it a purpose different from popping balloons.

Harcourt

"All right, Matt and Delia, it's your turn," Mrs. Brenner said. "Let's see, you've got levers, a pulley, wheels and axles, inclined planes—good. Let's see if it works."

"Matt, you drop the marble," Delia said. "It's mostly your idea."

"Hey, you're the shrewd engineer who solved most of the problems," I said. "Please, you do it."

Delia dropped the marble. It rolled down the screw. Then everything happened very fast. Train cars rolled. Dominoes toppled. Levers swung. Springs sprang.

And the balloon burst with a loud *pop*!

Our teacher, Mrs. Brenner, slid a transparency onto the overhead projector. "Our project this week will be to build something like this," she said.

The class gasped at a picture labeled "Balloon Popper." There was a balloon in it, all right, and a lot of other stuff. Some resourceful person had built a machine out of toys. There were blocks and balls, sand pails, and dump trucks. There were parts of building sets, train sets, and board games.

Harcourt

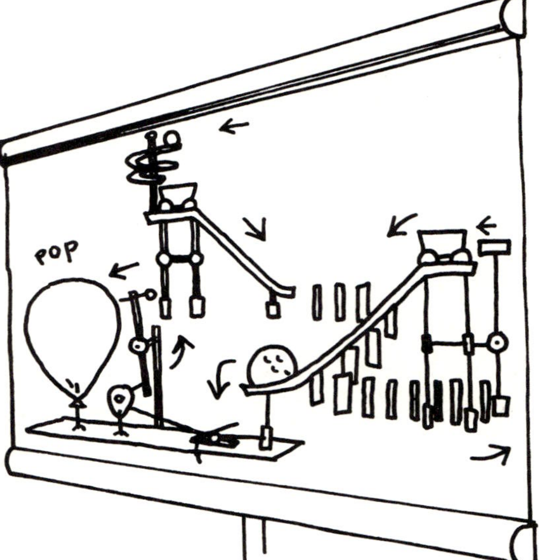

Each toy included at least one simple machine that made the next machine go. Simple machines such as pulleys and levers, are often parts of complicated machines. The balloon popper contained at least fifteen parts. They were rigged together in clever ways with rubber bands and string. At the end, a ball rolled down an inclined plane and tripped a lever made from a ruler. A sharp pin taped to one end of the lever came down and popped the balloon.

I thought it was the most inventive thing I had ever seen. It was totally cool.

Then I thought of it. "The last few dominoes don't have to be dominoes!" I said. "We'll use blocks shaped like dominoes. Each one can be slightly bigger than the last."

"And the last one will be heavy enough to trip the lever!" Delia said. I had never heard her so excited. "Matt, that's really inventive."

"Coming from you, that's a real compliment!" I said. "Let's try it!"

Harcourt

One step gave us more trouble than any other. Even with the extra weight, that lever didn't always fall far enough to send the train car rolling toward the ball. The dominoes just didn't hit the lever with enough force. Delia tried different ways of lining them up, but it worked less than half the time.

It was Thursday. On Friday we would have to run our balloon popper for Mrs. Brenner and the class.

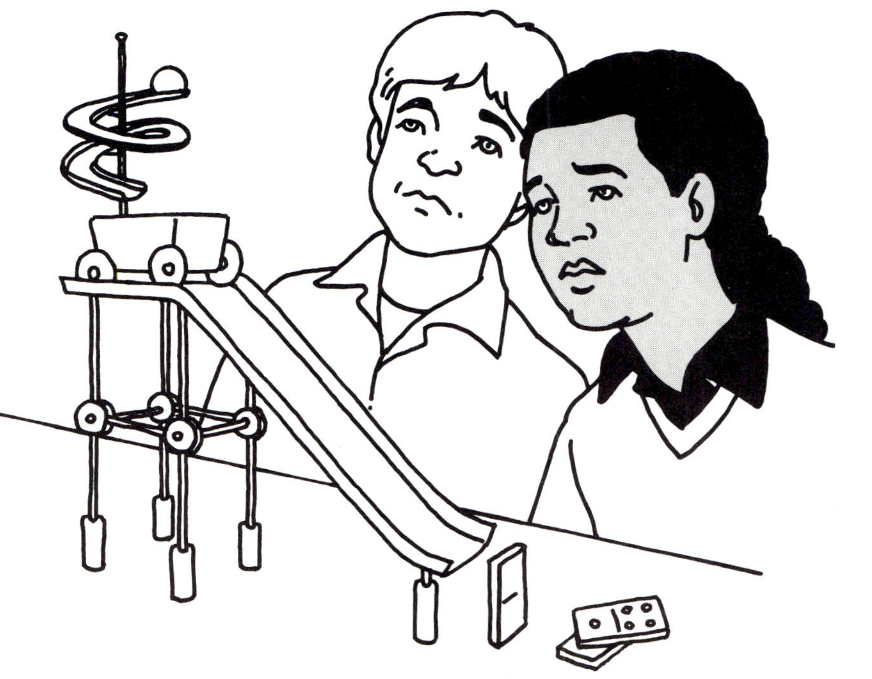

"You'll work in pairs," Mrs. Brenner said. "Don't worry—you won't have to be this enterprising. But you will have to use at least four of the six kinds of simple machines. And you'll have to show that your machine can actually pop a balloon."

I wanted to build a balloon popper with real quality. I was already starting to draw my design while Mrs. Brenner assigned partners. Then Mrs. B. popped my balloon.

"Matt Callan, Delia Miller—partners," she said.

I hardly knew Delia Miller. She had just moved here
from another state. I had the feeling she would not be
much help as a project partner—she never talked. I figured
this was probably because she didn't know much science.
Mrs. B. was pretty shrewd when it came to assigning
partners. Maybe she wanted me to help Delia.

After class, to spare Delia embarrassment, I told her,
"You don't have to do much with this. I'll do everything.
Look, I've already started."

Harcourt

I was discouraged. It didn't help that everyone in the
class was having the same problems we were.

"You have to be patient with projects like this," Delia
said in her soft voice. "This is how real machines are built.
You can have a top-quality design, but you still have to
test every part over and over. Sometimes you fail fifty
times before you make it work."

"How do you know so much about it?" I asked.

"From my dad," Delia said. "He's an engineer."

Harcourt

Each time we rebuilt and ran our machine, some parts worked, but never all of them. Sometimes the marble didn't land in the train car. "Let's place the parts more carefully," Delia said. "When it works, we'll mark the positions with a pencil." Sometimes the first lever didn't swing far enough to hit the train car. "Let's weight one end with blocks," Delia said. Sometimes we knocked over the dominoes by accident before everything was set up. Then we had to start all over again. "Let's leave gaps between the dominoes and fill them in when we're ready," Delia said.

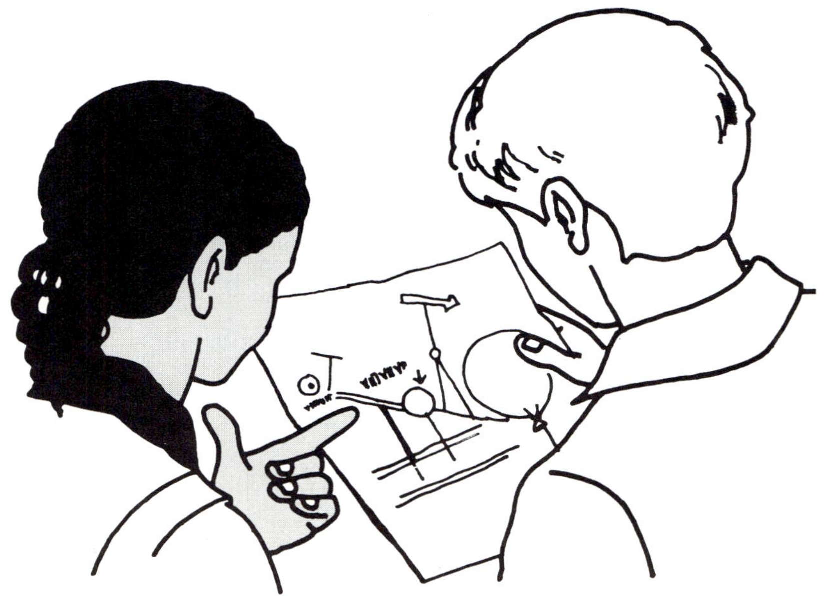

8

Delia studied my drawing. "You draw really well," she said softly. "But this won't work."

"What do you mean, it won't work?" I said.

"We'll need something heavier than a marble to open a clothespin," she said. "We could drop it from a greater height, but that would make it hard to aim."

The embarrassment was mine. I was about to come back with something smart, but Delia had paid me a compliment. Also, I saw that she was right.

5

All week, we planned and worked. We found some things in the classroom that we could use for parts, but we had to be resourceful about finding others. I had a ramp from a racing-car set that was shaped like the thread of a screw. We rolled a marble down that. The marble landed in a train car, sending it down a sloping track. At the bottom, the car knocked over a curving row of dominoes. The last domino hit a swinging lever mounted on a platform. The top of the lever hit another train car. It rolled down a track and knocked a golf ball off

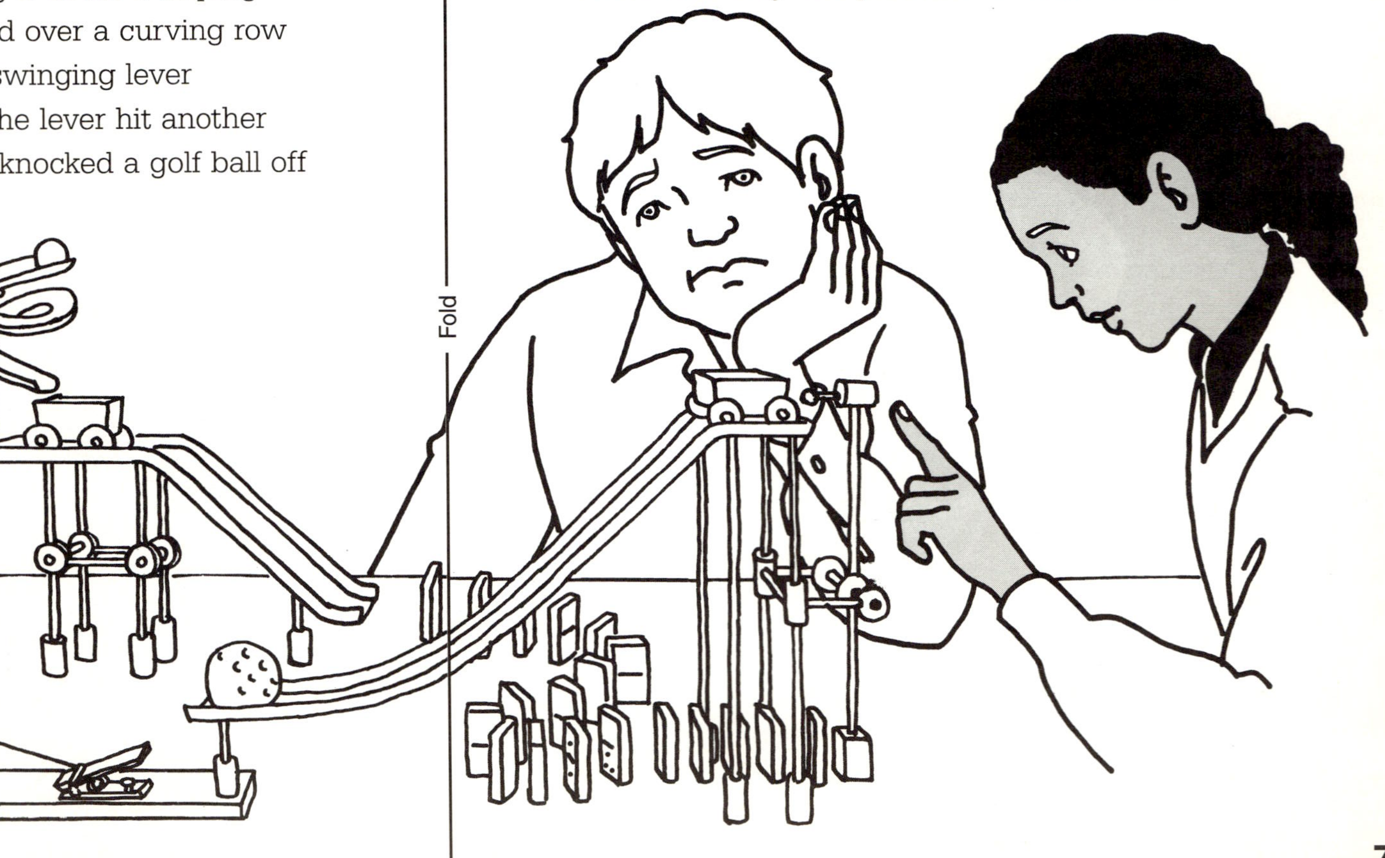

the end. The ball landed on a clothespin, springing it open. This released a string wrapped around a pulley, dropping another lever. A pin glued to the end of this lever popped the balloon.

It was the most enterprising design in the whole class. There was only one problem—it didn't work.

Harcourt

The Truest Treasure

by Mark Falstein

illustrated by Navin Patel

— Fold —

Harcourt

TAKE-HOME BOOK
Times of Discovery
Use with "The View from Saturday."

Answers:

1. the library 2. Mule's Hardware Store 3. Martin Luther King, Jr. Monument 4. Old Freight Shed and Barksdale Mall

Follow the Clues

Solve the clues as Nguyen and Megan did in the story. Use the map on pages 6–7 to find the places they went. Then number a sheet of paper from 1 to 4, and write the names of the places hinted at in the clues. The first clue has been answered for you. (The answers are on the back of this page.)

1. First clue (page 1)—the library

2. Second clue (page 4)

3. Third clue (page 5)

4. Fourth clue (page 10)

School-Home Connection Listen as your child reads this book aloud. Then, on the map on pages 6–7, have your child trace with a finger a route Nguyen and Megan could have followed from the library to Heritage Park.

Harcourt

There was band music, and speeches were made. Then the mayor announced the results of the treasure hunt. He thanked everyone who had given time, money, or goods to help make it work.

"And now," said the mayor, "let's get back to celebrating our freedom, which, as we know, is the truest treasure."

The crowd cheered. Then the fireworks began.

Nguyen was looking at the clock tower on top of the Barksdale Public Library. She was pedaling at a brisk pace and didn't see Megan until the last moment. "Hey, look out!" Megan yelled. Both girls braked just in time.

"Sorry," said Nguyen. "I wasn't looking. I just figured out a clue."

"It's okay," Megan said. "I wasn't looking either. Maybe I ought to get a clue myself."

Nguyen laughed. She showed Megan the slip of paper she had been given. It read:

Under my face and hands, a feast
you'll find.
Browse among my leaves and
feed your mind!

Harcourt

"Oh," Megan said, "the treasure hunt."

"Sure," said Nguyen. "Aren't you playing?"

"No, I don't know the town well enough," Megan said. "We just moved here."

"I didn't think I knew you," Nguyen said. "Do you go to Sawyer Middle School?"

"Not officially," Megan said. "I will this fall."

They introduced themselves. "N . . . Noyen?" Megan said, repeating the other girl's name.

"That's close enough," Nguyen said. "It's a Vietnamese name. We came here when I was a baby. Look, do you want to team up for the treasure hunt?"

"Sure, if it's not against the rules."

That evening the townspeople gathered at Heritage Park. Megan and her family joined Nguyen and her family for the picnic.

"This lemongrass chicken is great," Megan said. "Is that a traditional American Fourth of July dish?"

Nguyen's family laughed. So did Megan's parents.

"Sure, about as much as this Brazilian black-bean stew," Megan's dad said.

"Or this hamburger," said Nguyen's brother. "It's named for a city in Germany."

"Okay, okay," Megan said, laughing. "Give me a break. I'm new here!"

Harcourt

The girls rode to the spot they had guessed. Sure enough, another person in an Uncle Sam hat stood there. He bowed to them in a formal way and handed them their last clue.

Old and new, within a stone's-throw space,
Design a triangle beside my hiding place.

"I know where that is," Nguyen exclaimed. "So do I," said Megan. "I don't think I even need to look at the map again."

"There really are no rules," Nguyen said. "There's nothing formal about this hunt. Officially, there are no winners. The first ten finishers get little prizes, but it's mostly a way to raise money for charity. We do it every Fourth of July. Each clue takes you to where you get the next one. Then everyone gathers in Heritage Park for a picnic and fireworks."

Nguyen started pedaling, and Megan followed.

A woman wearing an Uncle Sam hat stood on the library steps. Nguyen explained to her how she had solved the clue. "You browse among the books," she said, "and a book has leaves." The woman smiled and handed her the next clue.

You'll find in this place that rhymes with
"jewels"
A hybrid plant among the tools.

"A hybrid plant," said Megan. "That's a plant that's bred from two different kinds. Maybe the clue means a plant nursery."

"But it has to rhyme with *jewels*." Nguyen took out her town map. "*Schools? Fools?*"

"Look," Megan said. She touched a name on the map.

The two girls looked at each other. "Of course!" Nguyen cried. "Let's go!"

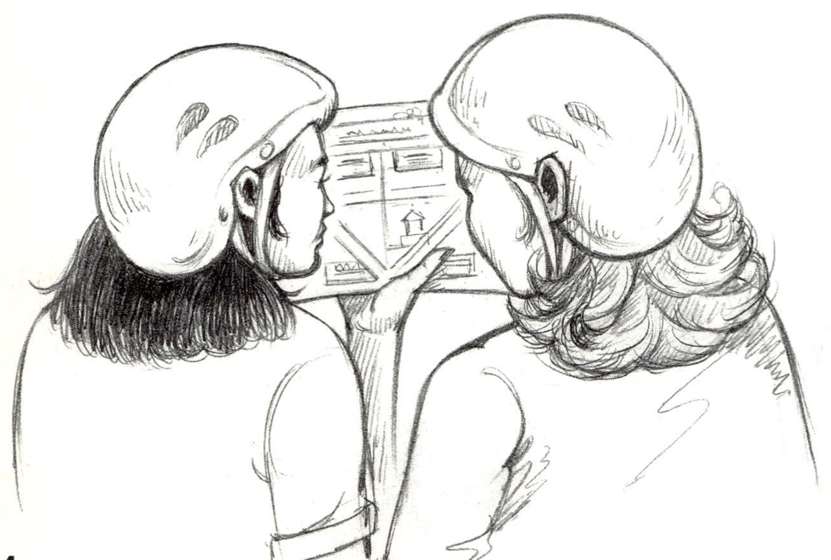

4

"Last year, my dad opened a bike shop," Nguyen said. "If you need a new bike or if one needs fixing, that's the place to go."

"Will you inherit the business someday?" Megan asked.

"No way," said Nguyen. "I just like riding bicycles. I think I'd like to run a bookstore, maybe—if I don't become a doctor or a soccer player."

"I'd like to be a dancer or teach Brazilian dancing," Megan said. "That's one of the things I'm going to miss here—the dancing."

9

Harcourt

Harcourt

"I do know one thing, though," Nguyen went on. "For a couple of years after we settled here, we were one of the families the treasure hunt helped."

"Really?" Megan was surprised that someone she'd just met would tell her something this personal.

"Sure. I get the idea that we didn't bring much more with us than the clothes we were wearing. But my parents worked hard. They raised vegetables to earn extra money. My brother and I spent our Saturdays at our family's vegetable stand at the Farmers' Market.

"Someone went to a lot of trouble to design this game," Megan said.

"Oh, the treasure hunt is very big here," said Nguyen. "My dad says it's something we inherit from the people who lived in Barksdale before us. It's like the freedom we celebrate on the Fourth of July."

"You know, this is my very first Fourth!" said Megan. "We've lived in Brazil since I was little. My dad's company just moved us back here."

"But you speak perfect English!" Nguyen said.

"So do you!" said Megan.

Megan had guessed right. The next clue read:

Our people fought King George the Third,
But this King moved us by his words.

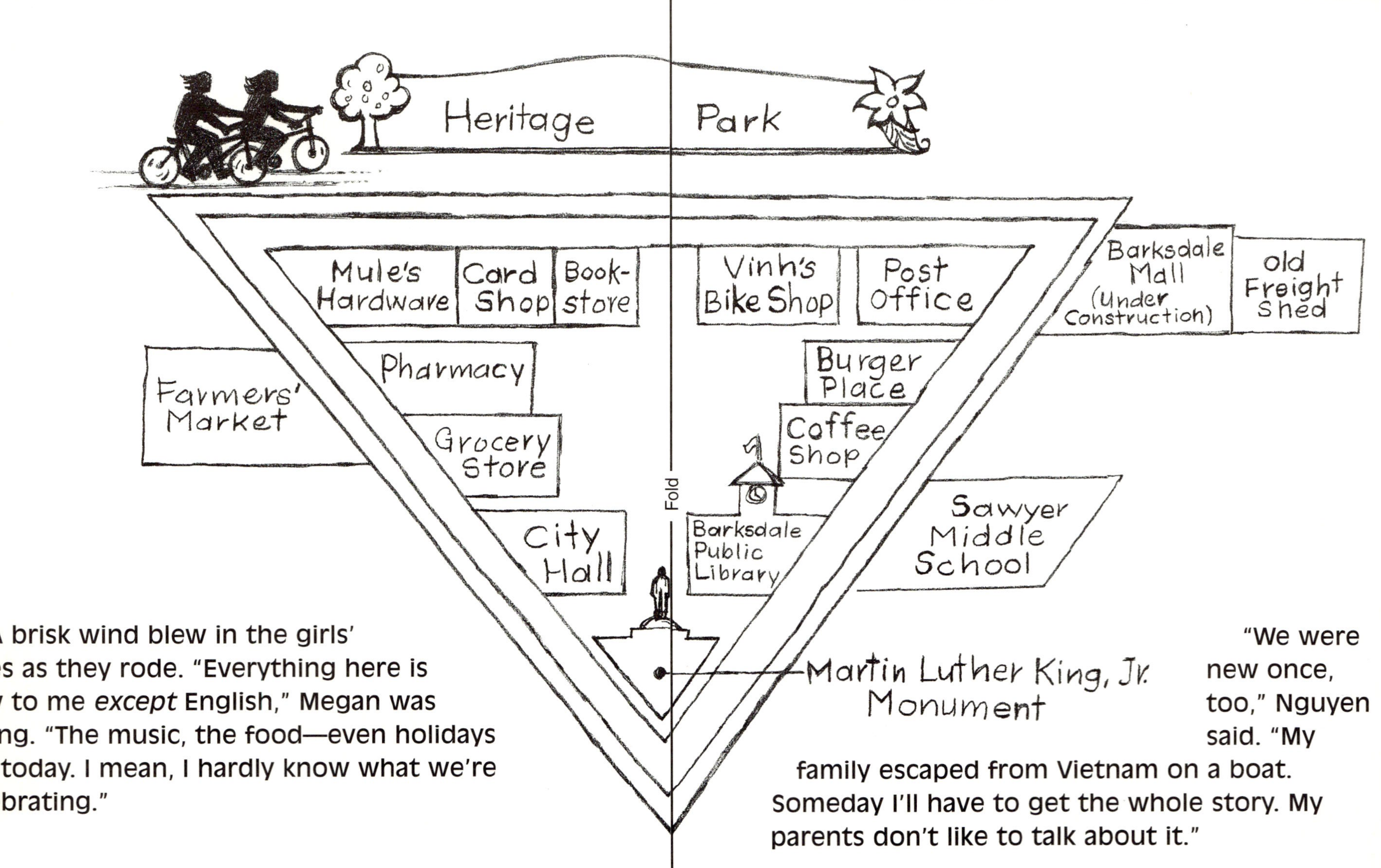

A brisk wind blew in the girls' faces as they rode. "Everything here is new to me *except* English," Megan was saying. "The music, the food—even holidays like today. I mean, I hardly know what we're celebrating."

"We were new once, too," Nguyen said. "My family escaped from Vietnam on a boat. Someday I'll have to get the whole story. My parents don't like to talk about it."

Harcourt

ALL-AMERICANS

by Elaine Roche-Tombee
illustrated by John Dollar

— Fold —

Harcourt

TAKE-HOME BOOK
Times of Discovery
Use with "Knots in My Yo-Yo String."

Answers:

1. catcher 2. shortstop 3. outfielder 4. Yankees 5. Mitchell 6. Sophie
7. winning 8. women

Name of city in New York State where Baseball Hall of Fame is located:
Cooperstown

Scrambled Baseball Words

Read each clue below. Number a sheet of paper from 1 to 8. On your paper, copy the blanks and the box or boxes shown for each scrambled word. Unscramble the letters to fill in the blanks. The letters in the boxes spell out the name of the city in New York State where the Baseball Hall of Fame is located. (The answers are on the back of this page.)

1. Player positioned behind home plate: ECCRATH

   ___ ___ ___ □ ___ ___ ___

2. Player who defends the infield near second base:

   THROOPSST ___ ___ □ ___ ___ ___ ___ □ □

3. Player positioned beyond the infield and between the foul

   lines: FOIDLTUREE ___ ___ ___ ___ ___ □ ___ ___ ___ □

4. Name of a major-league New York team: SKEAYNE

   ___ ___ ___ ___ ___ ___ □

5. Last name of the young pitcher who struck out Babe Ruth in

   a 1931 exhibition game: LEHCLIMT

   ___ ___ □ ___ ___ ___ ___ ___

6. First name of Racine Belles' fastest player: PIEHOS

   ___ □ ___ ___ ___ ___

7. Goal of all players on a team: IGNINWN

   □ ___ ___ ___ ___ ___ ___

8. People featured in a special 1988 exhibit in the Baseball

   Hall of Fame: NEMOW ___ ___ ___ ___ □

School-Home Connection Listen as your child reads this book aloud. Then attend a professional or school sporting event with your child.

Harcourt

In 1988 the National Baseball Hall of Fame opened an exhibit called "Women in Baseball." Many of the league's former players donated a memento or two. The exhibit quickly became one of the museum's most popular attractions.

The women who played in the league hold frequent reunions. They are often asked by reporters to talk about their playing days. Most of them have the same answer: "They were the best years of my life."

In 1943 the United States was at war. Millions of Americans were in the armed forces. Many women got a chance to work at jobs that had always been held by men. This is the story of some of those women.

Few groups of workers were immune to being drafted into the army. Baseball players were no exception. At the war's peak, more than 300 major-league players were serving their country. Some minor leagues stopped playing because they lacked players.

Americans wanted to be able to continue going to baseball games. Baseball was something to console them. Club owners scrambled to put together teams. A fifteen-year-old boy pitched for the Cincinnati Reds. A one-armed outfielder played one astounding season for the St. Louis Browns.

Philip K. Wrigley was the owner of the Chicago Cubs. He had a different idea for keeping baseball going. He started a new league—for women.

There had been women's baseball clubs as early as 1867. Lizzie Arlington had pitched in a minor-league game in 1898. Several women had played in exhibition games with major leaguers. In one such game, in 1931, seventeen-year-old pitcher Jackie Mitchell had struck out Babe Ruth.

The league played its last season in 1954. Its members could console themselves with the thought that they had truly been professional baseball players.

Some of the women went on playing on softball teams. Most found jobs outside of sports. Some used the money they had earned as players to go to college.

Many of the players married and had families. One was Helen St. Aubin, who had led the league in batting in 1945. Her son, Casey Candaele, later played in the major leagues.

Harcourt

After 1948 the All-American Girls' Professional Baseball League lost fans. There were many reasons for this. The league shifted players around from team to team. Rules and equipment were often changed in the middle of the season. There was no system for the development of new players. The league never caught on in the big cities.

One reason for the league's decline may have been television. People in the league's cities could now see major-league baseball without leaving home.

10

There were 40,000 women playing in softball leagues in 1943. Wrigley guessed he would have no trouble finding 60 players. That spring he held tryouts in Chicago. The best players were favored with invitations. Hundreds simply showed up.

Four teams trotted out onto the ball fields that first season. They represented Rockford, Illinois; South Bend, Indiana; and Kenosha and Racine, Wisconsin. Together they formed the All-American Girls' Professional Baseball League.

3

The players were called "girls" even though most of them were over eighteen. They came from all over the United States and from Canada and Cuba as well.

They were paid from $50 to $125 a week. Most players were factory workers and farm women, to whom this was good money. But some would have played for nothing.

The players did not like their uniforms. League rules made them play in skirts. Even in pants, players are not immune to injuries from sliding. Years later, however, many a former player still had her uniform, kept as a memento.

Alma "Gabby" Ziegler played second base for the Grand Rapids Chicks. Her playing and personality made her a team leader for eleven years.

Sophie Kurys was the league's fastest player. In 1946 she stole 201 bases for the Racine Belles and trotted home with the pennant-winning run.

Shortstop Dorothy Schroeder was only fifteen when she joined the Blue Sox. She played in the league for all of its twelve seasons. Charlie Grimm, the Chicago Cubs manager, said of her, "If she were a boy, I'd give $50,000 for her."

Harcourt

Harcourt

Some of the players became stars. Jean Faut of the South Bend Blue Sox was the league's best pitcher. She had 132 wins and lost only 62 games. Twice she pitched "perfect games."

Dorothy Kamenshek was a top hitter. She played first base for the Rockford Peaches. A former New York Yankees player called her "the fanciest-fielding first baseman I've ever seen—man or woman."

There were other rules. The women were supposed to be well behaved, off the field and on. A player might glare at an umpire, but she could be fined for back talk.

Many players did more than glare. The All-Americans' games were as tough and competitive as the ones the men played.

More than 175,000 fans turned out that first season. The Racine Belles were favored to win the pennant, and they did. But fans in all the league's cities turned out to support their teams.

More teams were added for the 1944 season. Attendance went up by more than half. In 1945 it doubled again. The league was an astounding success.

The big test came the following year. The war was over, and the major and minor leagues were back in full strength. The All-American Girls' Professional Baseball League continued to be successful. At its peak, in 1948, the league drew one million fans. Women's professional baseball seemed to be here to stay.

Harcourt

Harcourt

TAKE-HOME BOOK
Times of Discovery
Use with "The Marble Champ."

Answers:

```
            ¹C                    ²R
 ³C  R  O    S   S                 U
  H          U                     M
  A          N                     M
 ⁴M  I   T   T    S                A
  P          R                     G
  I          Y        ⁵F  U  M  E  D  D
  O                    L           D
  N        ⁶S  P  E    E  D
  S         O          X
 ⁷H  O   C  K   E  Y
  I         C          D
  P         E
           ⁸R  U   L   E   S
```

1 Down: COUNTRY
2 Down: RUMMAGED
3 Across: CROSS · 3 Down: CHAMPIONSHIP
4 Across: MITTS
5 Across: FUMED · 5 Down: FLEXED
6 Across: SPEED · 6 Down: SOCCER
7 Across: HOCKEY
8 Across: RULES

I CAN'T PLAY BASEBALL

by Eric Murray
illustrated by Bob Walker

"I Can't Play Baseball"
Crossword Puzzle

Copy the puzzle on a sheet of graph paper. Read each clue below and complete the puzzle. (The answers are on the back of this page.)

Across

3. See 1 Down
4. Baseball gloves
5. Showed anger
6. What a fast runner has
7. Game played on ice
8. Laws of a game

Down

1. With 3 Across, Jason's dad's sport
2. Searched by moving things around
3. Honor for a winner
5. Tightened, as a muscle
6. Popular sport around the world

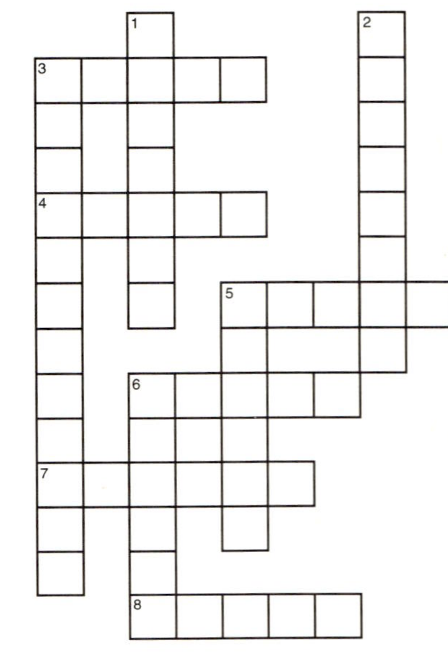

School-Home Connection Listen as your child reads the book aloud. Ask your child to describe his or her most memorable sports experience. Then share one from your own childhood.

Fold

Harcourt

Every time my son asks me to play baseball with him, I make excuses. "Sorry, I've got to clean the garage," I tell him. Sometimes it's "I've got bills to pay," or the old favorite, "I'm too tired."

Jason has trouble taking no for an answer. "Aw, come on, Dad, you can't be too tired for a little catch!"

"I'm suffering from exhaustion."

"Please, just half an hour? I'll get the mitts."

Of course, I usually agree—reluctantly. But when we play, I find myself glancing around. It's as though I'm worried someone will see me. In fact, I am.

I wish my son could see it that way. When Jason became interested in sports, I was quick to tell him that I didn't play baseball. But one day last summer, he rummaged through his grandparents' attic and found my old mitt. Since then, he's always after me to play with him.

Sometimes I ask him, "Why don't we just run around the field instead?"

Jason just gives me that look of his. "I don't think so, Dad," he says. "Come on, let me pitch you a few."

I can't play baseball. Never could. When I was growing up, everyone in my family seemed to have an instinct for the game. My dad had played minor-league ball in the Detroit Tigers organization, and he loved to talk about it. My two older brothers were stars from the playground through college. Even Mom played a pretty good second base.

As for me, I was hopeless. I ran past fly balls. I fielded grounders with my chest. I swung at bad pitches and let the good ones go by.

By the next season I was scoring mostly ones and twos. We won our league's team championship that year and the next.

After college I didn't run for years. But I took it up again in my thirties. It's a sport you can do all your life. You can do it almost anywhere, anytime you feel like it. You don't need a team to have fun or to stay fit.

Harcourt

My parents worried. My brothers fumed. A Murray who couldn't play baseball? It was like a cat who couldn't catch mice.

I laugh about it now, but there wasn't anything funny about it then. I have rummaged through my memory for my most embarrassing moments, and most of them happened on a baseball field.

Actually, it's not very funny even now.

Fold

Harcourt

In a cross-country meet, any number of people may run. You're awarded points for order of finish—one point for first place, two for second, and so on. The scores of each team's first five finishers are added together to get the team score. The team with the lowest score wins.

I placed fifth in my very first meet. I stood at the finish line and flexed and stretched my muscles. I felt like a world champion.

I had only one athletic skill—speed. I was the fastest kid in my class. In sixth grade the other guys matched me in a race against Henry Taylor. He was our team's lead-off man and center fielder. I can see Henry to this day, the way he flexed his leg muscles at the starting line. We raced around the ball field behind the school. He took the early lead, but I passed him three-quarters of the way along. I won easily.

It's too bad there's no "designated runner" in baseball.

4

I called Mom and asked her to send me my old track shoes. Then I started running every day. I trained all through the winter and into the spring. During summer vacation I was up at dawn every morning to run around the neighborhood.

By the time the next school year started, I could run six miles in 33 minutes. A week later, I was on the cross-country team.

9

Harcourt

Harcourt

One fall day I was walking in a park near the college. A bunch of young men ran by. They were wearing track suits, but there was no track. They were running over the hills and fields of the park.

That was how I found out about the sport called "cross-country." Men's and women's teams race across open land. The distances start at three miles and go up from there. It's a little like track—about as close as Thanksgiving dinner is to a snack at a fast-food stand.

I needed a sport I could call my own. Football? I was too small. Soccer? This was the 1960s. Then *nobody* in the United States played soccer. Basketball? In our city, hockey was the big winter sport.

You have to be able to skate to play hockey.

You may wonder why I didn't go out for track. Well, I did, in high school. I ran the mile. When the coach saw that I didn't drop dead of exhaustion, he had me try the two-mile run. I won a few races, but I quit the team after a year. I found running around a track boring. Besides, two miles was our longest race, and at two miles I felt as if I was just warming up.

In college a friend suggested I try wrestling. "It's not like you see on TV," he told me. "There are rules. You compete against guys your own weight." Reluctantly, I went with him to the gym.

The coach quickly decided that I had no instinct for survival. "Roll, Murray, roll!" he fumed at me. But it's hard to roll when you can't move.

Harcour

Harcourt

TAKE-HOME BOOK
Times of Discovery
Use with "Darnell Rock, Reporting."

Fold

Somewhere to Go

by Isabel Gallego
illustrated by Christian Slade

Your Own Op-Ed Piece

On a separate sheet of paper, write an op-ed piece on any issue that you'd like to be presented in a newspaper.

Fold

School-Home Connection Listen as your child reads this book aloud. Then talk about a news report from today's newspaper or a radio or TV broadcast. Ask your child whether he or she thinks the story was presented fairly. Ask what else might have been included.

It is Monday at Shawnee Heights Middle School. The staff of the school newspaper is finding it hard to concentrate. Everyone is talking about a story in Sunday's *Times-Clarion*. The story is about problems at nearby Shawnee Heights Mall.

"These store owners blame the noise and damage on 'young people' at the mall," Kim says. "My friends and I like to hang out there after school. We're not responsible for any violations of the law. But when they say 'young people,' they're talking about us."

1

— Fold —

Harcourt

And so we, too, would like the city council to put an item on its agenda. We'd like them to consider funding a community center in Shawnee Heights.

We could use a gym and a game room. A swimming pool would be nice, too. But mostly, we just need a place where we can hang out and talk.

Like the store owners, our parents pay taxes in this community. We have a right to ask for something back. Maybe the store owners could put up part of the money if the city would provide the rest. They would be removing what they see as the problem at the mall. And we would have somewhere else to go.

12

Harcourt

"Right, it's not fair," says Alfred. "They want an ordinance keeping out people who aren't customers. Well, I'm a customer, sometimes. I buy clothes there. I go to the movies and to the food court. Are they going to kick me out when I'm just there to meet friends?"

"Mr. Klein, you told us a reporter should get both sides of a story," says Wendy. "This reporter only got the store owners' side. She didn't talk to any of the 'young people' they're blaming for all the violations."

"Well," says Mr. Klein, "if you feel that way, why don't you write an op-ed piece for the *Times-Clarion*?"

We'd also like an apology from the *Times-Clarion*. A news story is supposed to report both sides of an issue. Your reporter presented only the store owners' side. Why didn't she talk to any of the "young people" at the food court? Why didn't she postpone judgment until we had a chance to explain our side?

If she had, she might have asked us why we gather at the mall. And this is what we would have told her: because it's somewhere to go. Shawnee Heights has few recreational facilities for young people.

Harcourt

First of all, we'd like an apology from you and the other store owners. We know that some young people, especially teens, get noisy. We appreciate that you don't want your property damaged or stolen. But it is grossly unfair to hold people responsible only because of their age.

The great majority of us who gather at the mall are well behaved. We meet our friends, shop, and buy snacks. Why do you lump us all in with those few who cause trouble?

"A what?" several students ask.

"An op-ed piece. It's short for 'opinion-editorial,' or 'opposite of the editorial.'"

Mr. Klein opens the daily newspaper. "See, here's the editorial page of the *Times-Clarion*. You all know what an editorial is."

Dwayne nods. "Sure, it's opinions of the paper's editorial staff about current events and things."

"Right. Now, next to it is the op-ed page. This is where the paper prints other people's opinions. Most of them are well-known writers or public figures. Here's an article by Senator McIntyre. It explains where she stands on the issue of funding for schools."

"But most papers also have a free-speech column. The *Times-Clarion* calls it Open Forum. Anyone can write on any subject. This man wants the city council to postpone their vote on the new bike path. He thinks the ordinance is unfair to property owners."

"Why would the *Times-Clarion* print anything *we* wrote?" asks Amanda.

"Why wouldn't they—if it's effective and well written?" Mr. Klein answers.

The story quoted Mr. Lamar Bell, of Bell's Camera Shop. He implied that the people responsible for the "rowdy behavior"—mostly loud talk—are also doing the stealing and vandalism. He urged the city council to pass a law preventing "young people from using the mall as a gathering place."

"If the council does not place this item on its agenda, stores will close," Bell said. "We pay taxes in this community, and we want something done."

Well, Mr. Bell, we are the "young people" of this community. We'd like something done, too.

Harcourt

Harcourt

The students' article appears in Monday's issue. Here's what it says.

Which Young People?

Recently a story appeared in the *Times-Clarion* about problems at the Shawnee Heights Mall. Store owners were angry about stealing and property damage. They were also concerned that "rowdy behavior by young people, especially around the food court," was driving away customers.

"Here's our chance to tell those store owners what we think of them," Alfred says.

"Sure, if it makes you feel better," Mr. Klein says. "But if you want it to be *read*, write about the issue, not people. The paper won't print an 'attack piece.' You can't write something that's false and meant to damage someone's reputation."

Harcourt

The students work on their op-ed piece that day and the next. They all contribute ideas. Then Dwayne writes the first draft.

"This is too long," Amanda says. "I checked out the Open Forum columns for the past week. They're all 500 words or less."

"But these are all important ideas," Dwayne says. "What can we cut?"

"Figure it out," says Mr. Klein. "A shorter piece can often be a more effective piece. And you'll want to get it in soon, or the mall story will be old news."

The students finish their article on Wednesday. They send it by mail to the *Times-Clarion*.

The paper's editors receive dozens of Open Forum articles every week. They can print only six each week. They cannot spend a lot of time making their choices. A well-written piece by middle-school students catches their attention.

Harcourt

TAKE-HOME BOOK
Times of Discovery
Use with "Number the Stars."

Answers:
Pennsylvania—"Like many other people in Pennsylvania, Jonathan . . ."
(page 3); 1776—the year independence was declared (page 3); fall—when
apple cider is made (page 8)

Fold

The Root Cellar

by Karen Stamfil
illustrated by Anita DuFalla

Where and When?

This story gives clues to its setting. Look at the map below, and find the area in which the story takes place. On a sheet of paper, describe the setting. Write the name of the place, the year, and the season. Explain where in the story you found the answers. (The answers are on the back of this page.)

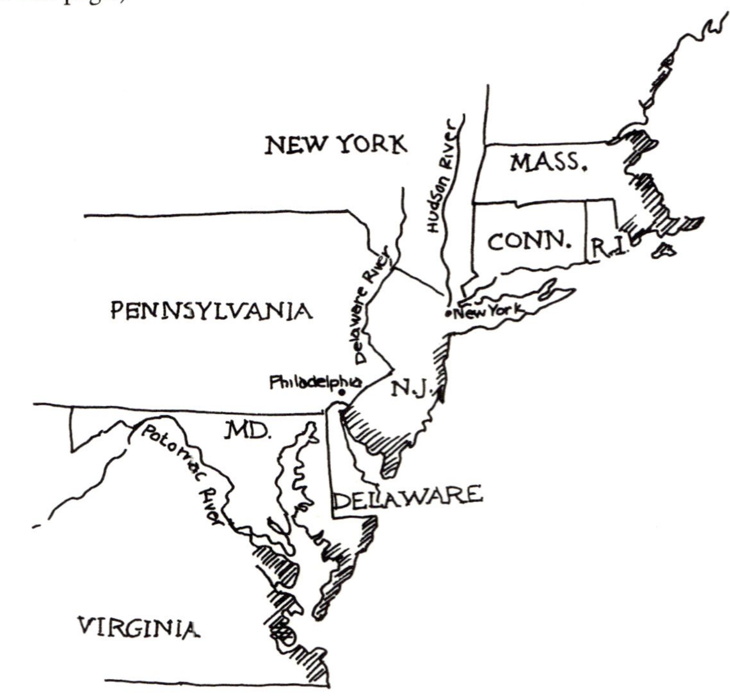

School-Home Connection Listen as your child reads this book aloud. Then ask your child who his or her favorite character was, and why.

Fold

Harcourt

Later that evening, Jonathan sat down with his family. "I am sorry I put you all in danger," he said.

"We live in dangerous times," Hannah said.

"I see that now," said Jonathan, "though I think your mother saw it some time ago."

"But it all came out all right," Susan said.

"Yes, it did," said Rebecca, "this time." She hugged her husband. "I hope Jacob is safe," she added.

Jonathan didn't answer. He was thinking that this country would someday belong to young men like Jacob Sutter and young women like his daughters. It would belong to them in a way that it had never belonged to him and Rebecca.

Jonathan Harris saw young Jacob Sutter running up the road. Jacob looked frightened. He stopped and tried to pull himself together as he neared the gate.

"Friend Harris," he gasped, "I beg you for help."

"What is the matter?"

"Soldiers are after me—King George's men," Jacob said. "Please, is there a place I can hide?"

Jonathan had many questions, but Jacob was a good lad and a neighbor.

"Come," he said soothingly, "You may hide in my root cellar. But you must tell me what the trouble is."

Harcourt

"I was digging a well when I saw them coming," Jacob said. "I barely had a chance to get away. They think I've been spying on the Hessians'[1] camp and passing secrets to General Washington."

"Jacob, Jacob!" said Jonathan. "Why would they think a thing like that?"

"Because I *am* a spy," Jacob said belligerently. "I want to end this occupation of our country. What are you going to do—turn me over to them?"

---

[1] **Hessians** German soldiers who fought on the British side in the Revolutionary War

"You're planning to slip across to New Jersey and join General Washington," Jonathan said.

"How did you know?" Jacob asked in surprise.

"It's what I would do if I were young," Jonathan said belligerently. "It's time we all stood up for our rights as Americans."

"Why, friend Harris!" said Jacob. "I never guessed you supported our cause!"

"I didn't before," Jonathan said. "I do now. Now go, and stay safe."

Jonathan waited until it was almost dark. The pigs had left little of the apple mash that had hidden the door to the root cellar.

"Here is a little food and money," he said to Jacob. "It won't be safe for you to go home. The British will be watching your house, but I'll get word to your family."

"I owe you my life," Jacob said.

"It's a fair trade," said Jonathan. "My family and I shall owe you our freedom."

"What do you mean?" asked Jacob.

Harcourt

Like many other people in Pennsylvania, Jonathan had not taken a side in the war. He had paid little attention in July when the Congress in Philadelphia declared independence. Just let me mind my farm, he had thought.

Even though Jonathan was unwavering in his support of a friend, young Sutter exasperated him.

"You're living dangerously, Jacob," he said. "Of course, I'll not turn you over. You'll be safe here."

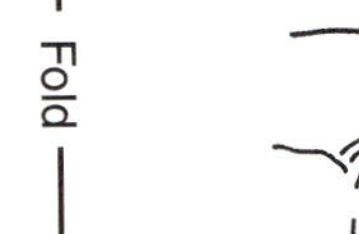

Harcourt

Rebecca Harris waited inside the house. "What made you decide to be a hero?" she asked disdainfully.

Jonathan was surprised at his wife's anger. "I'm just helping a neighbor," he said.

"Jacob Sutter's problems are his own," Rebecca said. "What if redcoats come here looking for him? You've put our daughters in danger."

"Rebecca, what would you have me do?"

"Sir, there's no sign of Sutter," a soldier reported.

"We shall move on to the next farm." The major stood up. "You," he said, snapping his fingers at Jonathan, "you seem a loyal subject of the king. There may be a reward in it for you if you help us find him."

The soldiers marched out. Rebecca and Jonathan hugged their daughters. "It's all over, it's all over," Rebecca said soothingly.

No, thought Jonathan, it's just beginning.

Harcourt

"There is fresh apple cider my husband made this morning," Rebecca said. "Would you like some?"

Major Stitt wrinkled his nose. "Yes, and I notice you have left the mash[2] outside your door for your pigs," he said disdainfully. "I should think you would notice the smell."

Although the major's attitude exasperated her, Rebecca was unwavering in her calm. "Hannah, get the gentleman bread and meat and cider," she said.

"You," the major said to Susan, "be a good girl and clean the mud off my boots."

[2] **mash** The soft pulpy mass left after apples are squeezed to make cider

Rebecca gave a sigh. "It's a brave and good thing you've done," she said. "Even if it means the occupation of my house by King George's men."

"Occupation!" Jonathan looked at his wife in surprise. It was the same word Sutter had used. "You favor the rebels? You never spoke of it!"

"You would not have listened."

Before he could reply, Rebecca swept their daughters before her into the parlor. "Come along, Hannah and Susan," she said. "We have candles to make."

The British soldiers came an hour later. They were commanded by a Major Stitt.

"We seek Jacob Sutter, a neighbor of yours," the officer said.

"He is not here," Jonathan said. "You may look for yourself."

"I don't need your permission," Major Stitt said. "You men, search the house! Turn over every bed. The rest of you, search the barn."

The soldiers marched into the house in their muddy boots. The major turned to Jonathan.

"Sutter is a rebel spy," he said. "If he's here, give him up now. It will go hard for you if you don't."

Jacob is a friend, Jonathan thought, but I wouldn't even give an enemy over to this one!

"I haven't seen Jacob Sutter," he said.

The major settled down in their best chair. "You," he said to Rebecca, "fetch me food and drink."

Harcourt

October 17

by Mark Falstein
illustrated by B. Gita

— Fold —

Harcourt

TAKE-HOME BOOK
Times of Discovery
Use with "Summer of the Swans."

Answers:
1. shake   2. Ada   3. Yen   4. fire   5. doorway   6. Oakland   7. ravine
8. doctor   9. routine   10. compulsion   11. Vic   12. broken

Name of Carin's city: **San Francisco**

Earthquake Puzzle

Read each clue at the left. Number a sheet of paper 1 to 12. On your paper, copy the blanks and the box shown for each clue. Use the clue to fill in the blanks. The letters in the boxes spell out the name of Carin's city. (The answers are on the back of this page.)

1. What Carin felt the house do

2. Female neighbor's first name

3. Male neighbor's last name

4. What Carin saw to the west

5. What you should stand under during an earthquake

6. City where a road collapsed

7. Deep, narrow valley

8. Where Carin's mom was

9. Regular way of doing something

10. Feeling of being forced

11. Name of Carin's brother

12. What Carin hoped the gas line wasn't

School-Home Connection Listen as your child reads this book aloud. Then discuss with your child the things you can do to prepare for an earthquake or other emergency.

Harcourt

I remember that afternoon well!

I had checked in with the Yens next door when Vic and I came home from school. Then I went to my room to do my homework. I was under some compulsion to finish it because I had to fix dinner. Mom was at the doctor's and would be home late. Vic was cleaning his room and watching TV. I could hear its murmur through the door.

I had the radio on. An announcer was reading news headlines. It was a Tuesday, just after five o'clock.

When the rumbling started, at first I thought it was a truck passing on the street. Then it got louder. The house began to shake as if some giant had picked it up and was playing with it.

We were having milk and cookies. Other neighbors had stopped by to check on us. Mr. Yen checked the gas line. It seemed OK, "but we should wait for the fire department to turn it back on or the gas fumes might engulf us," he said. "Carin, you did great. You must have paid attention to those school earthquake drills."

"I guess I did," I said.

Mrs. Jaynes had been a little girl in San Francisco during the great earthquake of 1906. She was telling stories about it when Mom finally came home.

"Wouldn't you know? I was in the doctor's office when the quake hit and the lights went out!" she said. "I had to get dressed in the dark and walk down nine flights of stairs. Then I walked all the way home!"

We all laughed. We were glad we were safe. And I knew we all had stories we would tell for a long time to come.

Harcourt

The announcer stopped talking. Then he said, almost in disbelief, "This is an earthquake, isn't it?"

I heard Vic scream in anguish. Just then, the power went off.

I felt as if I was climbing a hill as I groped toward the door. A *moving* hill.

"Vic, get under the big table!" I yelled.

"Mommy!" he wailed.

I pulled Vic under the table. You're supposed to get under something solid. A doorway is best. But the hallway to the front door seemed like a huge expanse of ground. A ravine could open up in the floor and engulf me before I got there.

I invited Mrs. Jaynes down to our apartment.

"Let's make her some tea!" Vic said.

"That's a nice idea, but there's no gas for cooking," I said.

"Let's build a campfire!"

"I don't think so, Vic."

"Thank you, Carin and Vic, for coming to my rescue," Mrs. Jaynes said. "I don't know how long I might have lain there if you hadn't helped me."

Harcourt

"Mrs. Jaynes!" I called.

"Mrs. Jaynes!" Vic echoed.

I heard a faint cry. "In there!" I said.

Mrs. Jaynes had fallen during the earthquake. "I'm all right, I'm all right!" she said as I helped her up. "No bones broken. But my china—just look at it! My mother's china, which came all the way *from* China!" she said in anguish.

I hugged Vic until long after the shaking ended.

I thought of the earthquake drills we had regularly at school. I had hardly paid attention to them. They didn't seem real. This was real enough!

There was a routine you were supposed to follow. What should I do first?

The gas line. You were supposed to shut off the gas in case the line was broken.

"Vic, come with me." I hoped he couldn't hear my voice waver.

"I'm scared," he said. He was crying softly.

"Then you'll have to stay here while I go."

"No!" He scrambled to his feet and followed me next door to the Yens' apartment.

I told Mr. Yen about turning off the gas. We all three went to the basement. I found the lever and Mr. Yen pulled it. No one in the building would be able to cook until the line was checked, but there wouldn't be an explosion.

Back upstairs, I checked the water in our apartment. It was running. There didn't seem to be any damage to the apartment. Then I tried the phone. It wasn't working.

We went across the street to Aziz's Market. I bought batteries for the radio and flashlights. I bought snacks that wouldn't need cooking or refrigeration.

4

Back home I seemed to be under a compulsion not to panic. Darkness was falling, and I read to Vic by flashlight. I kept the radio on. The news was grim. I was glad Vic didn't understand. It seemed like an adventure to him now.

Then I heard a soft thumping on the ceiling.

"That's Mrs. Jaynes!" I said. "She may need help!"

Ada Jaynes was 93 years old. Until that moment, I hadn't thought of her. Now I didn't waver. I grabbed the key we kept to her apartment, and Vic and I dashed upstairs.

9

Harcourt

"Listen," I said to Vic. "We're just going to follow our regular routine, all right? I'll fix you a peanut-butter sandwich and some milk for supper. Then I'll read you some books until Mom gets home."

"OK," said Vic. "She'll be home soon, right?"

"Sure," I said, trying to hide my disbelief.

8

Several neighbors were on the street, talking quietly. Someone had a radio on. There were reports that part of the Bay Bridge was down. Across the bay, in Oakland, a main road had collapsed.

Where was Mom's doctor? Not in Oakland, I hoped.

Sirens wailed in the distance. Smoke was rising not far to the west, beyond the hill.

"Come on," I said to Vic. "Let's take a walk."

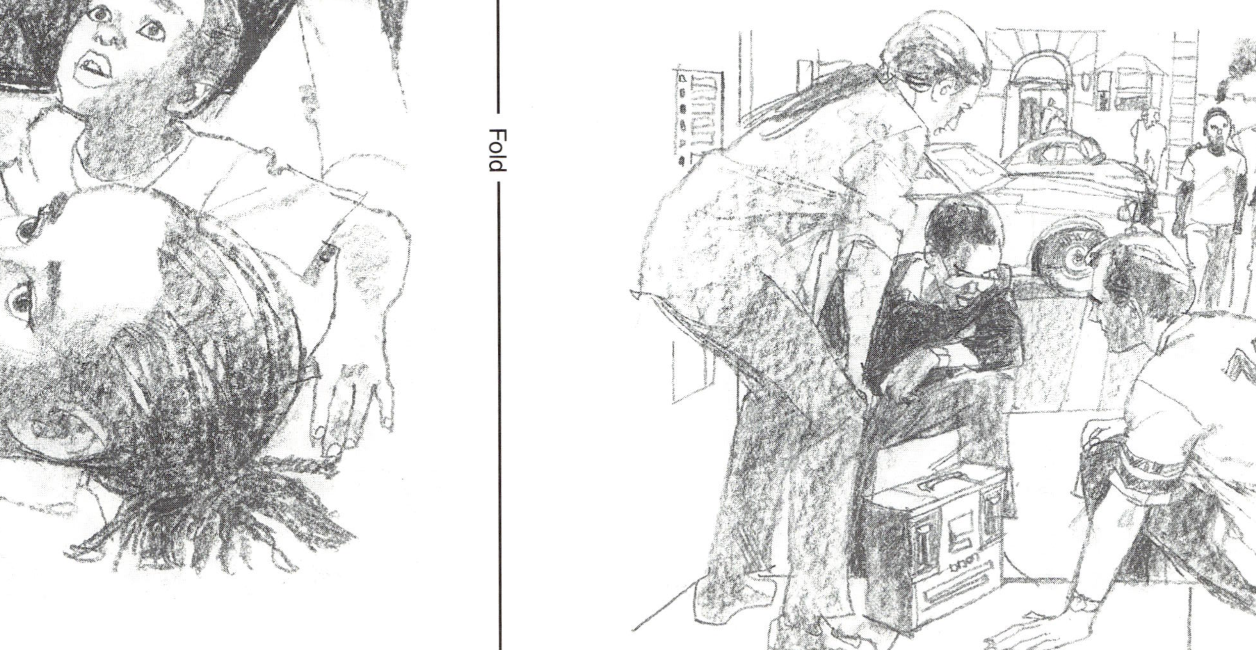

5

We walked up the hill. From the top, we could see across the expanse of San Francisco. No ravine had opened to swallow up the city. But there were buildings on fire to the west, past the library. On Franklin Street a brick front had fallen off a house. Traffic was a mess everywhere we could see.

Harcourt

Harcourt

TAKE-HOME BOOK
Times of Discovery
Use with "Old Yeller."

Answers:
1. wedges   2. pound   3. yarns   4. romping   5. Sancia
Another word that means *jumped suddenly:* **pounced**

The Girl Who Spoke Dog

by Elaine Roche-Tombee
illustrated by Holly Cooper

Word Scramble

Read each clue at the left. Number a sheet of paper 1 to 5. On your paper, copy the blanks and the box (or boxes) shown for each clue. Use the clue to fill in the blanks. Then unscramble the letters in the boxes to spell another word that means "jumped suddenly." (The answers are on the back of this page.)

1. Pieces of wood, metal, or other material that are thick at one end and thin at the other

2. Where Mrs. Rovig got Rocky

3. Another word for *stories*

4. Playing in a rough, tumbling way

5. The name of one of Sofia's dogs

Fold

School-Home Connection Listen as your child reads this book aloud. Then have your child describe his or her favorite pet or a pet your child would like to have.

Harcourt

On Saturday, Mrs. Rovig came to pick up Rocky. She had her son, Ben, with her.

I explained how you get a deaf dog to obey commands. I also gave her Dr. Bacon's number. While we talked, Ben made Rocky sit, come, and heel, using my signals.

"You can use a different signal if you want to teach him to shake hands," I told him.

"Does this mean we can keep him?" Ben asked.

"Oh, yes. We can keep him," Mrs. Rovig said. "Thanks to the girl who speaks dog."

"Hello, is this the girl who speaks dog?"

I hate that nickname, but I answered, "Yes, I'm Sofia Estévez."

"Great," said the voice. "I'm Mrs. Laura Rovig. I've been hearing some very interesting yarns about you. They say you've never met a dog you couldn't train."

I let that one go by. It's true, but some people would take it as bragging if I said so myself.

"I do train dogs, yes."

"Great. I've heard that you do wonders. I'm looking for someone to train a puppy. In fact, I'm desperate."

I gave the woman my address and told her to bring the dog over.

That was how I met Rocky.

He was lunging at the end of a leash, pulling her behind him. He was big for a puppy. He looked to be half Australian Shepherd. Which half was anybody's guess.

"I got him from the pound," Mrs. Rovig explained. "My son wanted a dog. He's six," she added. "I can't get him to behave. The dog, not my son. Down, Rocky, down!" she said as he pounced on me.

"You see?" she said helplessly. "My landlord says I have two weeks to train him. If I can't, I either have to take him back to the pound or move."

Harcourt

Rocky was romping in the muddy yard. I put the leash on him and held it tight. Then I held a piece of food over his nose and moved it back over his head. Just for form's sake, I said "Sit!"

Rocky sat.

I held him on a long leash. I faced him with my right hand down at my side. Then I brought it across my body to my left shoulder as I jerked the leash. "Come!" I called.

By Wednesday he didn't need the leash. He was coming on the hand signal alone.

Harcourt

The next morning I called Dr. Bacon, our vet.

"I think I have a deaf dog," I said. "Is there some way I could find out for sure? And do you know anything about training a dog that can't hear?"

"Bring the dog into my office on Monday," Dr. Bacon said. "We'll have someone check it out. As for training, yes, there are a few things you can try. . . ."

I told her to leave Rocky with me and not to worry. Then I told her my rates.

"Your parents won't mind an extra dog around?"

"My mom likes what I do. She says I've 'found my calling.' I'm planning to be a vet when I grow up."

"That's wonderful." Mrs. Rovig took two rubber wedges out of her purse. "Here," she said.

"What are these for?"

"Stopping your doors so he won't escape."

When she left, I had to stop him from charging after her.

It was Saturday, so I started right away.

Training dogs is easy. First, you have to have a feeling for them. As far as that goes, those yarns about me are true. But a lot of it is just common sense.

Say you're teaching a dog to sit. You just say "Sit!" in a commanding voice while pushing down on its back. When it does the right thing, you say "Good boy (or girl)!" and give it some food. After a while, even the dumbest dog gets it.

Rocky didn't get it.

4

Every dog I'd ever met was afraid of thunder. Rocky just pounced and licked my hand as if he wanted to play.

"Rocky?" I said.

Then it hit me. I bent down and shouted as loudly as I could.

"Rocky!"

A clap of thunder shook the house. Sancia whimpered. Sailor tried to hide under a chair. Rocky just stood there panting, with his tongue hanging out.

9

Harcourt

We keep the dogs in a closed-in porch off the kitchen in bad weather. Sancia and Sailor barked and whined as if the world were ending. I comforted and petted them, and then went back for Rocky.

I remembered the wedges Mrs. Rovig had given me. I was about to put them in the door when I realized something.

Rocky wasn't scared.

It was the same with "Come!" You're supposed to jerk the leash as you say it so the dog knows it should move toward you. Rocky would come, all right. He'd come lunging right past me and pull me down. But he wouldn't come on command.

To teach a dog to heel, you first get him to sit next to you. Of course, Rocky would sit only when he got tired of romping. Then you do "sneak-aways." If the dog doesn't stay beside you, you run in the opposite direction. Then you snap the leash hard and say "Heel!" The dog learns he's supposed to stay with you.

Rocky stayed with me, all right.

I tried giving him commands in Spanish, but that didn't work either.

Rocky was a sweetheart. He didn't bark. He got along fine with my own dogs, Sancia and Sailor. He made me laugh, the way he went charging after tennis balls. He was a funny, shaggy puppy. He would make someone a good blanket on cold winter nights.

If he made it to winter.

After a week I was worried. I was making no progress. Mrs. Rovig called me twice. I didn't want to tell her how badly things were going, but I couldn't lie to her. I felt sorry for her and her son—and for Rocky.

That business about not barking, that should have been a clue.

On Friday afternoon the sky darkened early. Just before bedtime a thunderstorm hit.

"You'd better bring the dogs in," Mom said.

Harcourt

TAKE-HOME BOOK
Times of Discovery
Use with "Shiloh."

Answers:

```
    1C
 2N U I S A 3N C 4E
    R       W   R
 5R E C K L E S S      6N
    E       W   S      A
    N       A  7T A P E R E D 8D
    T       R   R       E
       9R I 10D G E   11G L O W E D
          M       W       R
          M
       12R A N G E R S
```

Crossword Puzzle

Copy the puzzle on a sheet of paper. Read each clue below and complete the puzzle. (The answers are on the back of this page.)

Across

2. Something that annoys
5. Dangerously careless
7. Became smaller toward one end
9. Long, narrow, high ground
11. Shone
12. People who patrol a park or forest

Down

1. Flow of water
3. Clumsy
4. High point of a 9 Across
6. Like a mountain trail (not wide)
8. Animal seen by 10 Down
10. Shannon's sister

School-Home Connection Listen as your child reads this book aloud. Then talk about what your child should do if an emergency situation arises.

Harcourt

"A helicopter pilot saw you and radioed us for help," one of them said. "What are you doing here?"

"Mudslide," Shannon gasped. "Road blocked. My father and sister—"

Later, Shannon had trouble remembering the rest.

They took her to a hospital and brought her father and Emma out by helicopter. They would have to come back for the car when the road was cleared.

Meanwhile, the fire was out.

"You've done a very brave thing," said her father, and Shannon was glad he didn't say much about it.

"Daddy, when can we go camping again?" asked Emma. Shannon was wondering the same thing.

They could see the smoke rising from the valley, but Shannon wasn't worried.

"Forest fires aren't likely in May," she said. "Everything's still wet."

She pointed to the stream they were crossing. The current was swollen from rain and melted snow.

"I don't know, Shannon," her father said. "There's a saying—'where there's smoke, there's fire.'"

"True, but it may not be smoke at all. I think it's just air pollution from cars on the highway."

It was the last day of their camping trip. The car was packed, but Shannon had asked for one more hike.

Harcourt

Shannon loved camping. She loved sleeping in a tent and seeing the night sky bright with stars. She loved the smell of campfire smoke and the taste of camp cooking. Best of all, she loved being on a trail, where everything was quiet and still. Everywhere she looked, there was something to delight her eyes.

This year, at last, her sister Emma was old enough to enjoy it, too. Emma had always been a nuisance on camping trips. She had to be watched all the time. Emma still got tired on hikes, but this time she had had fun. She even remembered to be quiet when a deer crossed in their path.

Now the going was very slow. Here and there a rock or a tree root made progress awkward. As Shannon pushed her way up the last few yards, she started saying to herself, "I *think* I can, I *think* I can." The thought almost made her laugh.

There. There was the crest of the trail. There was only one more bump to get over—

"Hold on!" cried a voice above her. "We're coming!"

Rangers were waiting on the fire road. They pulled her, exhausted, into a truck.

Harcourt

Above the campground the road tapered to a narrow trail. "I made it up this trail this morning," Shannon reminded herself. But she had been fresh then. She remembered to stop and drink from her water bottle frequently.

A helicopter flew overhead, going toward the fire. Shannon stopped and waved her arms. She yelled as loudly as she could. But the helicopter flew on.

The trail crossed the stream. It switched back steeply up the ridge on the other side. "The fire road is right below the top," she told herself.

A ranger was waiting near their car. "We were about to go looking for you," he said. "There's a fire on the ridge to the west. We're sending everyone down the mountain just to be safe. You're the last ones."

"Thank you," Dad said. "We'll leave right away."

"Take it slow," the ranger said. "You don't want to get reckless on that narrow road."

In the back seat Emma was making up a song about the deer they had seen.

"Well, Dad, you were right about the fire," Shannon said.

"You're a good woodswoman," her father said, "but don't take chances with fire. It's just a nuisance now, but with this wind picking up—"

"Dad, look out!" Shannon yelled.

Her father was already braking the car. A slide of mud, rocks, earth, and trees was tumbling down the hill toward the swollen stream below.

4

How long had they driven down the dirt road? It couldn't have been more than 20 minutes. How fast could her father have been driving? It couldn't be too many miles back to the campground—could it?

Her arms were aching long before she reached the campground. When she got there, she stopped and called out. She got no answer.

The smoke above the ridge glowed red. Now and then, flames licked the sky.

9

Harcourt

Harcourt

"Okay," he said. He gave her a smile and a hug. "You go get help. I'll stay with Emma."

He didn't say "Good luck." It wasn't necessary.

It was uphill nearly all the way. Shannon pushed her way along the narrow road with her strong arms and shoulders.

"This is no different from being in a ten-mile race," she told herself. "I bet it's not even that far."

8

Dad began backing up the car, slowly and carefully. But the slide had already tapered off.

Dad gave a deep sigh. "Well, this is awkward," he said. He reached into the glove compartment for a phone. "Emma, you okay back there?"

"Sure," Emma said. "Daddy, is there any paper in the car? I want to draw a picture of the deer."

"Sure, honey," Dad said. He jabbed at the phone. "Well, isn't this lovely," he said. "It's not working."

5

Shannon was thinking. Her father didn't want to scare Emma, but she knew he must be worried.

They couldn't get past that slide, not even on foot. They couldn't back up or turn around. There was a swift current to their left and a forest fire to their right.

The rangers might not know about this slide for hours. Everyone would be busy with the fire.

"Dad, there's a fire road above the campground," Shannon said. "Remember, we crossed it on our hike? People will be using it to go fight the fire."

"We could start walking back that way," Dad said. "I'd have to carry Emma."

"I could get there quicker myself," Shannon said.

"No way," her father said. "We stay together."

"It's the only way," said Shannon. "Trust me, Dad. I won't do anything reckless. I can get there."

Her father followed Shannon's glance. A curtain of smoke rose above the ridge.

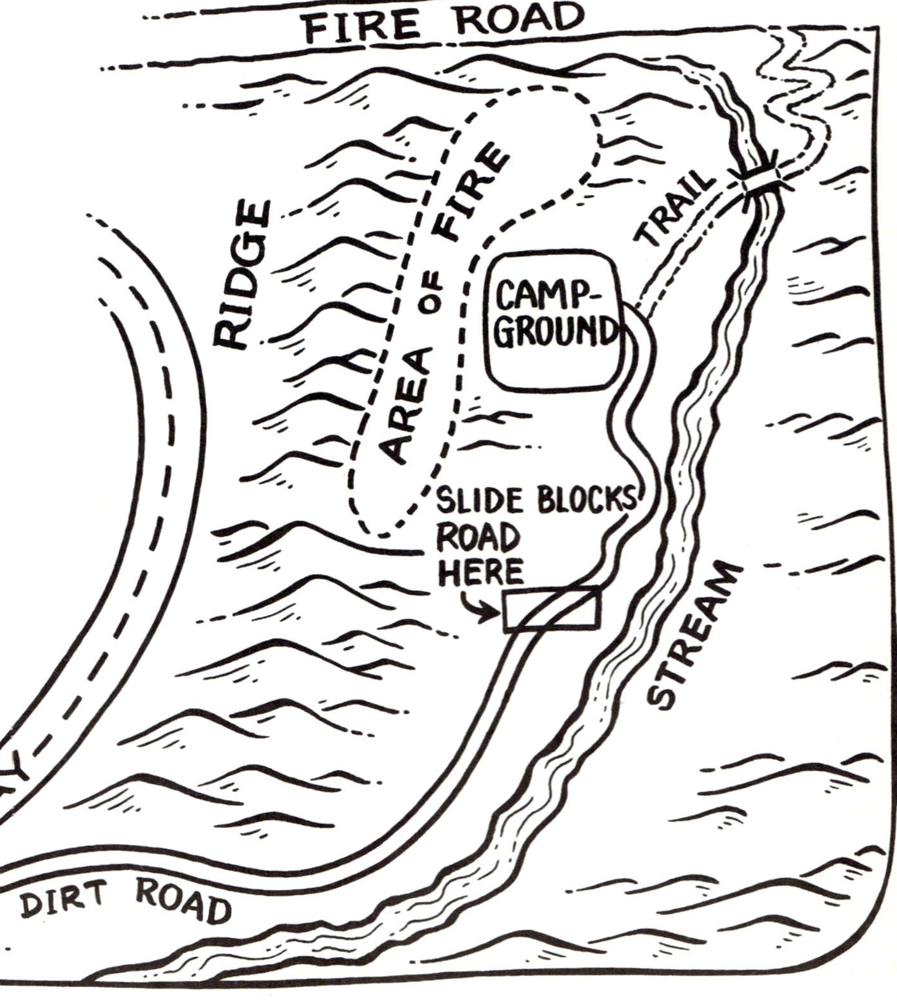

Harcourt

TAKE-HOME BOOK
Times of Discovery
Use with "Flood: Wrestling with the Mississippi."

Floodplain

by Isabel Gallego
illustrated by Holly Cooper

An Adaptation for Television

Suppose you were writing "Floodplain" as a play for television. Choose one of the scenes from the story. On a sheet of paper, describe in detail what the cameras would show. Choose actors from the class to play the characters involved.

Fold

School-Home Connection Listen as your child reads this book aloud. Then have your child explain who his or her favorite character is and why.

Harcourt

David gave Marie Dr. Espina's message. She hugged him before she left. "If the rain doesn't start again, we have a good chance," she said.

"More than a good chance," Tom Nathan said. "Welcome," he called to the volunteers, "and thanks for coming." He began sending them to stations along the levee.

"Autumnhorse, are you still here?" Tom said an hour later. "You've certainly been doing an adult's job. Why don't you go home and get some sleep?"

"I'll be okay," David said. He yearned for sleep, but there would be plenty of time to rest after the river had crested.

12

It was the full moon of May. David Autumnhorse stood on one of the levees that protected Saddlersville from the White River. He was awed by what he saw.

Normally, the White River lay far below. A small pool down there was David's favorite fishing spot. Now muddy brown water swirled almost at his feet. Trees, boards, and other debris were carried along by the rushing stream.

1

Harcourt

"It crested in Lyman this afternoon at 27 feet," David said to his sister, Marie. "If the rain doesn't let up, we're in real trouble."

"Well, it isn't seeping through the levees yet," Marie said. She had driven up that morning from Dallas, where she was a nurse. She gave the angry river another glance. "Come on, let's find Tom Nathan and see how we can help."

2

David hurried back outside. He splashed down the street toward the river. Two school buses turned the corner, spraying water. David saw them pull up across from the levee.

Men and women poured out, carrying tools. There were even a few boys and girls his age. They were volunteers from towns safely above the floodplain who had come to help.

11

Harcourt

The crowd became silent and awed by the sound of rain. Then a cheer went up in the gym. It took David a moment to realize what had happened. The drumming and splashing sound outside had stopped. For the first time in four days and nights, it wasn't raining!

Tom Nathan was the basketball coach at the high school. He was captain of the volunteers on this part of the levee. All of his team was there helping out.

"We've got human chains going to the top of the levee," Tom said. "David, you fill these sacks with sand. Pass them along to the next person in the chain. Good to see you here, Marie. Are you up to tossing 40-pound sacks around?"

"Of course," Marie said, a little indignantly.

"Just making sure," said Tom. "Go join that chain over there."

"Tom, we just got a call from Finleysburg," said Mrs. Chastain. She ran a restaurant in town. "The reservoirs there are about to flood. They'll have to open the gates and let some water out."

Tom frowned. "That's bad," he said. "Okay, let's speed it up," he shouted. "Carol, call all the radio stations in the upland towns. Tell them to put out a call for volunteers. We're going to need all the help we can get."

4

The gym felt like a time-out zone. People were resting and gulping down sandwiches and lemonade. One corner had been fitted out as a first-aid center. Dr. Espina looked up and recognized David.

"David, did I hear right that your sister is in town?" the doctor asked.

"She's out on the levee," David said.

"See if the crew can spare her," Dr. Espina said. "I could use some more trained help here."

9

Harcourt

"We're going to need another layer of bags here,"
Tom Nathan called. "The water is seeping through in
places." David heard the strain in Tom's voice. He began
to work even harder.

Tom threw a glance his way. "Autumnhorse, you look
like you could use a break," he said.

"I'm okay," said David. He felt proud that the coach
had called him by his last name, as if David were one of
his basketball players.

"Go on, take a break," Tom said. "There's food and
lemonade in the high school gym."

David worked faster. He shoveled until he yearned for
rest, and then he shoveled some more.

He thought of his parents' hardware store in town
and his grandparents' farm a few miles away. He
had helped his parents board up the store and pile
sandbags around it that morning. His grandparents had
left for higher ground, taking with them whatever their
trucks could hold. David remembered the stories they had
told him about the floods of earlier years.

"Why would anyone farm on a floodplain if there are floods so often?" David had asked Grandpa Ed.

"Because a floodplain has the best soil for growing crops," his grandfather had said. He had pointed across his wheat field. "All this black earth was a gift of the river. The river gives, but it takes away, too."

"Our people have farmed along the White River for 2,000 years," his grandmother had added. "We dug reservoirs for the dry times, but we let the river flood the fields when it wanted to." She gazed at her sturdy farmhouse and brightly painted barn. "You gain something when you build to last, but you lose something, too," she said. "In the old days, we'd just move the village to higher ground and wait it out."

Harcourt

THE FIRST ARTISTS

by Neil K. Armfast
illustrated by Anita Dufalla

<hr>

Fold

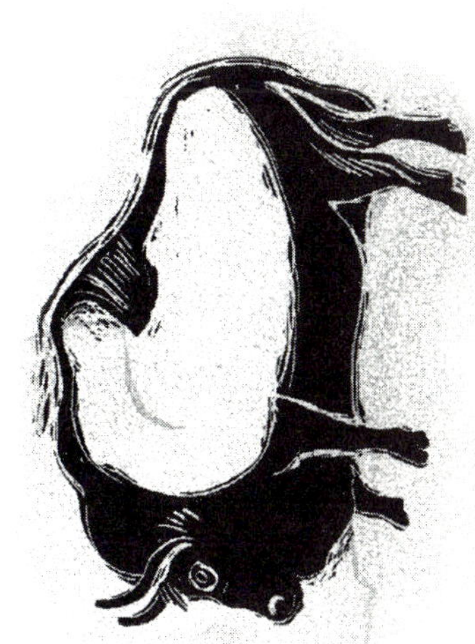

Harcourt

TAKE-HOME BOOK
Times of Discovery
Use with "Stone-Age News."

Be a Cave Artist

Think of what you know about Stone Age people and how they lived.
Then make your own "Stone Age cave drawing" on a separate sheet of
paper. Make it show something of Stone Age life.

School-Home Connection Listen as your child reads this book aloud. Then ask
your child to tell you what facts about Stone Age art he or she found most
interesting and why.

Harcourt

Cave art may have been a sociable activity. Hand marks and footprints of men, women, and children have been found in painted caves. Were some images "male" and others "female"? Were some favored by young people and others by old? Did many people create art, or was it the specialty of a few? We will probably never know.

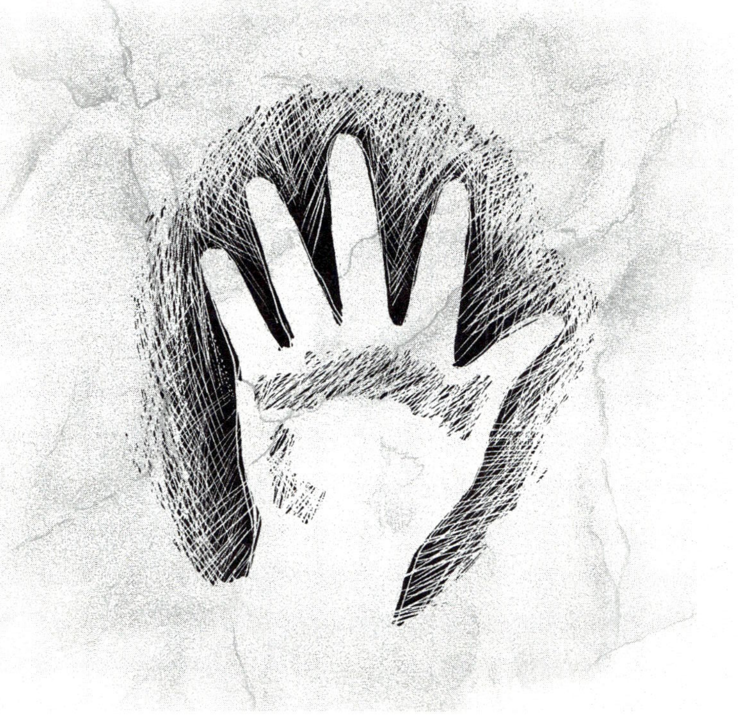

Fold

Jean-Marie Chauvet [shō•vā′] is an official in a small town in France. Late in 1994 he and two friends were exploring a cave near the town. They moved carefully, guided by lamps strapped to their foreheads.

Suddenly a mammoth appeared on a wall. The three explorers moved their lights around slowly, scouring the wall with light. They were astounded by what they saw. The walls were carved and painted with animals. There were horses, buffalo, and rhinoceroses. There were lions, mammoths, and a red-spotted bear. In all, there were more than 300 animal images in what is now called the Chauvet cave.

Jean Clottes [klôt] was called in. He is a French scientist whose specialty is Stone Age art. Clottes declared the paintings to be the real thing. "It's great art!" he said. He compared the Chauvet cave to the famous painted caves of Altamira [äl'tə•mir'ə] and Lascaux [la•skō']. But the Chauvet paintings would reveal even more surprises.

Cave artists did not paint with brushes. Sometimes they used their fingers. Sometimes they put the paint in their mouths. They would blow or spit it onto cave walls.

The paints were made from colored earth mixed with animal fat. Stone Age paint-mixing tools have been found near the Niaux [nyō] cave in France. Bits of paint were still on the tools. They matched the paints used in the cave.

Harcourt

Harcourt

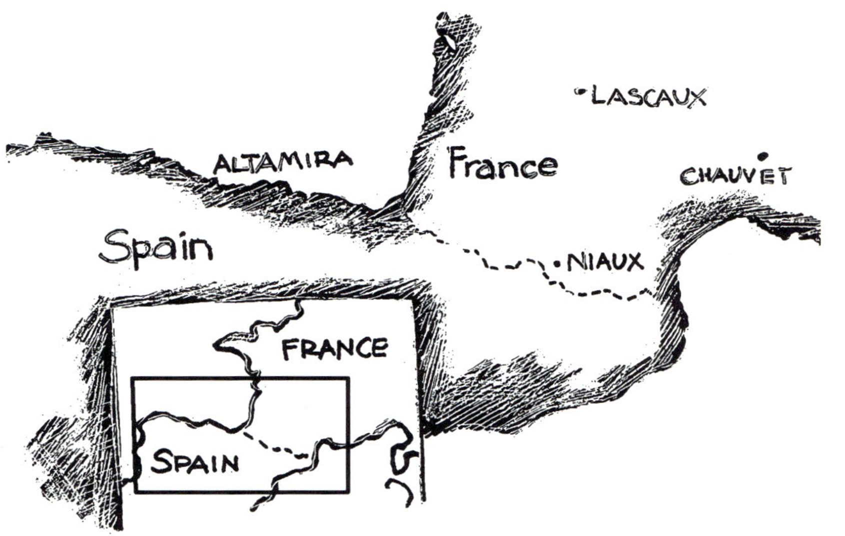

We can only guess what the painted animals and other images meant to Stone Age people. Were the images a record of people's dreams? Were they pictures of their wishes and fears?

In some caves, paintings were made thousands of years apart. They may have meant different things at different times to different people.

Many Stone Age art treasures have been found in southern France and northern Spain. The Altamira cave in Spain was the first to be discovered, in 1879. Its paintings of animals seemed so expertly done that at first many people believed they were fakes. Later, dating methods indicated that they were thousands of years old.

In 1940 the cave of Lascaux in France became the second great Stone Age "art museum." Since then, more than fifty painted caves have been discovered.

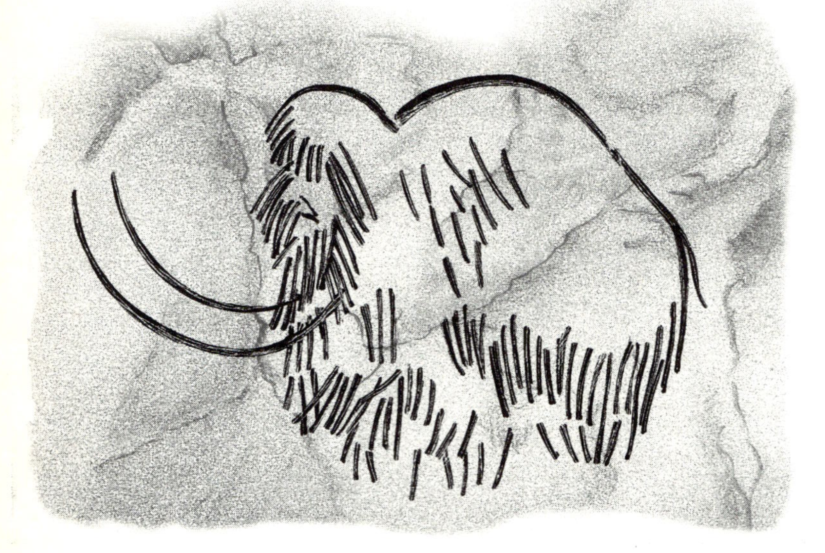

Jean Clottes applied dating methods to the Chauvet paintings. The results astounded him. Most painted caves date from what scientists call the Magdalenian [mag′də•lē′nē•ən] period. Magdalenian culture is believed to have flourished thousands of years ago.

The Chauvet paintings come from a much earlier and colder time. They are believed to be many thousands of years old. They are the oldest paintings ever found in Europe.

It also appears that people never lived in the Chauvet cave. This is true of many caves in which paintings have been found. Stone Age humans did use caves for reliable shelter. But they nearly always slept, ate, cooked, and worked near the mouths of caves. Paintings are often found deep inside caves. Sometimes they are in dangerous, hard-to-reach places.

Harcourt

Harcourt

In the places where art flourished, what did it mean? People today create art for pleasure and to express ideas. What ideas might the cave artists have been expressing?

Scientists thought ancient people painted animals in hopes of gaining power over them or increasing their numbers. But, despite carefully scouring cave walls, scientists rarely find paintings of common food animals, such as reindeer. They often find paintings of animals not hunted for food. In the Chauvet cave, for example, the animals that appear most frequently are rhinoceroses and lions.

The Chauvet discovery stirred new interest in an old question: Why did early humans create art?

Most scientists today believe that modern humans arose in Africa thousands of years ago. Humans then spread across Asia, Europe, and Australia. Art began to appear in Australia, southern Africa, southern Europe, and northern Asia.

It is possible that people in these different places "invented art" at about the same time. But few scientists believe it happened this way. Most think the newfangled art spread from one place to the next.

How could this have happened? Early humans were probably as sociable as people are today. When groups met, they often traded with one another.

They traded ideas as well as goods. One group might show another a newfangled idea such as how to skewer food for cooking. They would skewer the meat on a piece of bone and roast it over the fire. This might give the other group the idea to try it, too.

Art must have been a powerful idea, to spread so quickly. Yet in many parts of the world, no ancient art has been found. This could mean that people in those places didn't care about art.

But it might also mean that they carved on wood or painted on animal skins. Their art would not have lasted very long. Painting on rock and carving on bone were more reliable ways of preserving art.

Harcourt

TAKE-HOME BOOK
Times of Discovery
Use with "Ancient China."

Fold

The Serai

by Isabel Gallego
illustrated by Robert Dellinger

A Letter from the Trade Route

Suppose that you traveled the trade route with Sen. On a separate sheet of paper, write a letter to a friend, describing one of your exciting travel experiences.

Fold

School-Home Connection Listen as your child reads this book aloud. Ask your child how one might tell when this story takes place. Ask your child to find a hint that suggests how to find out.

Harcourt

But best of all was the colored glass. There were jars and bottles of all shapes and sizes. They were made of every color of the rainbow.

The glass would be packed carefully in straw and carried thousands of *li*[1] to China. There it would bring a fortune in the city markets.

In his mind Sen chose a special dark green bottle that he wanted as a present for his mother.

Then the traders sat down. The bargaining began!

---
[1] **li** a Chinese unit of measure, about one-third of a mile

12

"What do you *mean*, he won't let us trade?"

Sen's brother frowned. With a wave of his hand, he signaled Sen to be quiet.

Sen and his brother, Ah Chun, couldn't be sure who among these strangers understood Chinese. They knew they should not let them know what they were thinking. But they had been on the road for a year! They had crossed baking deserts and towering mountains to reach this land called Persia.

And now this Persian administrative official would not let them trade. Had they come all the way for nothing?

1

The traders were in a *serai*. The Persian word meant "palace," but it was nothing like the emperor's elaborate palace in China. It was a resting place for caravans.

There were Romans from the far end of the earth in the serai, too. They did not speak Chinese. The Chinese traders did not speak their language.

However, the traders of both groups spoke a little Persian. The Persian official was talking to them now.

Finally Sen's brother, Ah Chun, turned away. He signaled to his group to join him outside.

The next day the Chinese unloaded their goods. They spread out roll after roll of fine, pale yellow silk.

Then the Romans unloaded their goods. There was gold and silver. There were pearls and diamonds. There was cloth colored richly purple by a secret dye.

Harcourt

Harcourt

Sen watched his brother talk with the Persian. He saw the official nod slowly, and then eagerly.

"You're a born trader, Sen," Ah Chun said. "Everyone has agreed to your idea. The Persians will be our official interpreters. That will earn them a fine fee. It's not as much as they would get by trading, but this way they get something. There will be other caravans to make them rich."

"It's like this," Ah Chun explained to Sen. "We've never traded directly with Romans before. It's amazing to meet them. Usually we don't go this far west and they don't come this far east."

"That's because usually someone along the road is at war with someone else," another Chinese trader named Yan added.

"Right," said Ah Chun. "Or there's famine, or the inhabitants somewhere want to grab a share. There's always some danger. That's why we bring our silk here from China and trade with the Persians. The Romans trade their goods with the Persians, too."

"And the Persians trade with both of us, and everyone makes money," Yan said.

"Right again," said Ah Chun. "Only now, for the first time, there is peace all along the road. There is no famine anywhere. We can trade directly with the Romans. We'll make more profit that way."

"Except the Persians don't like being cut out of the deal," Yan said with a laugh. "Well, too bad for them!"

"We'll work something out," said Ah Chun. "If we don't, everyone loses. But it may take some rather elaborate bargaining. We may be here a while."

"It means 'silk people' in their language," Yan said, laughing. "It's not an insult."

"You've done well," Ah Chun said. "It's hard to understand Persian. Honored Grandfather told me that in his day the trade was silent. We'd set our goods on the ground. They'd set down as much of their goods as they thought they were worth. If we agreed, we'd just pick them up. If not—"

"Brother, excuse me, but that gives me an idea!" Sen said. He spoke to Ah Chun for a few moments.

"You know, that might work!" Ah Chun said. "Let me talk to that administrative person."

Harcourt

Suddenly the Romans' caravan master smiled at Sen and greeted him in Persian. Sen knew a few words of the language. He told the man his name and where he came from.

The man called himself Joseph. He came from a place called Antioch. It was one of many cities ruled by the emperor of the Romans, whose name was Trajan.

That was all Sen understood. Joseph kept calling the Chinese "Seres." The name puzzled Sen.

Sen knew his brother would not have brought him here if the road were not at peace. Still, trade went on even when there was great danger and risk.

"All the inhabitants of the world desire silk," Ah Chun had told him. "Only we Chinese know the secret of making it. And every civilization has something to trade for it. We only have to get it there."

Every day the journey had brought wonders. Now Sen was staring at the camels of the Roman traders. They were taller than any he had ever seen—and they had only one hump!

Sen wanted to be a trader like his brother and his uncles. He had been delighted when they invited him on this journey. Like them, he had walked all the way. They had used camels only for carrying precious goods.

The adventure had begun even before they had passed beyond the Great Wall and the terraces planted with wheat. But Sen now realized that China was only a small part of the world.

"We Chinese once thought we had the only civilization," Ah Chun had said. "Just 300 years ago, the Han emperor knew nothing of India or Persia. The Greeks and Romans were not even a story to us!"

Now Chinese silk reached all those places. Sen had met Indian traders in the markets of Bactria. He had seen their jade and ivory and tasted their spices.

Although he was enjoying this adventure, Sen sometimes wondered when he would see the terraces near Loyang and taste his mother's cooking again.

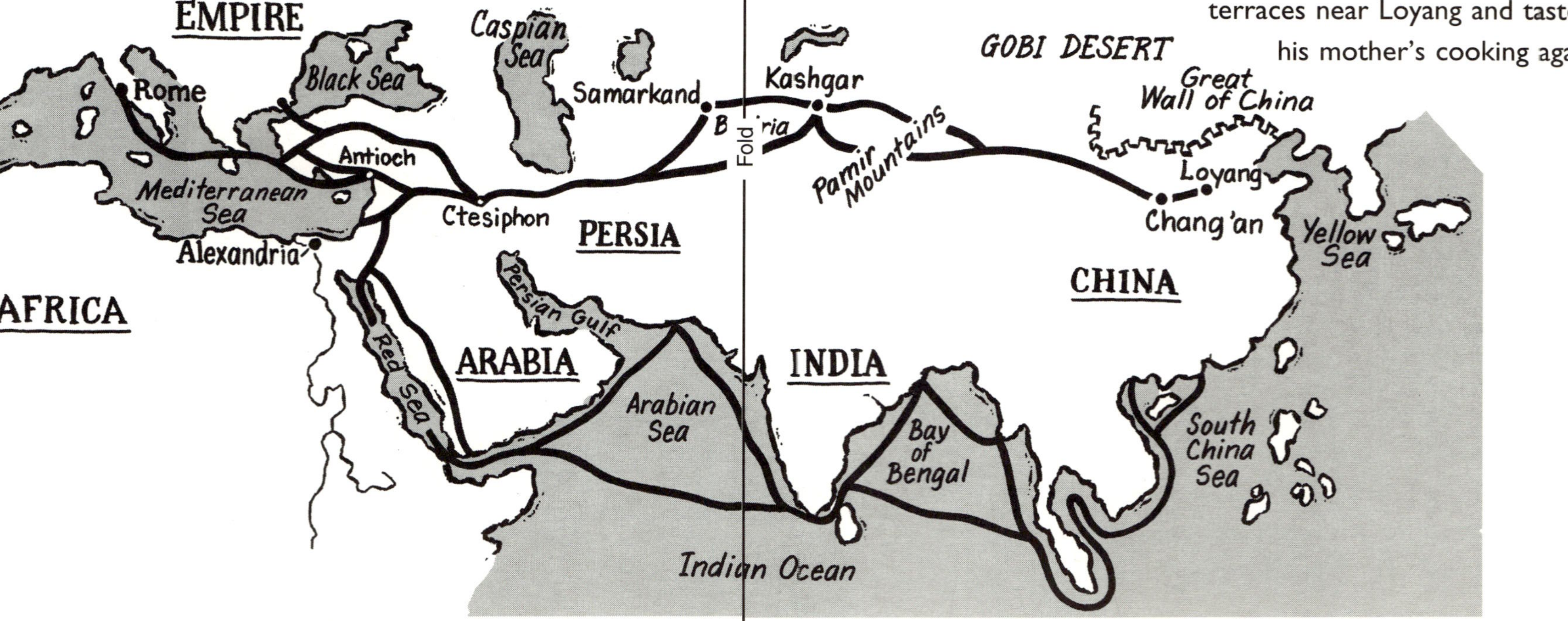

JOURNEY TO KUSH

by Mark Falstein

illustrated by Anne Olds

TAKE-HOME BOOK
Times of Discovery
Use with "Pyramids."

Harcourt

Dear Diary

Suppose Candace had taken a diary with her on her trip. What might she have written in her diary the day she arrived at Meroë? On a separate sheet of paper, write a diary entry for Candace, telling what she thinks about her adventures.

DATE ____

____

____

____

____

____

____

____

School-Home Connection Listen as your child reads the book aloud. Then share with your child memories of an eventful trip you have taken.

Fold

Harcourt

By now Candace Moore was used to the bouncing. The truck was moving along at 25 miles per hour, but the paved road had ended many miles back. They were following the tracks of previous traffic along the Nile River.

"There's a train," Uncle Leo had told Candace. "But it's always crowded, and it's not very reliable. That's why Anwar is driving passengers by truck. This is the best way to travel through Kush, unless you want to go the old-fashioned way—by camel."

"Kush?" Candace asked, grinning at her uncle. "I thought it's been called Nubia for the last seventeen centuries."

"True," said Uncle Leo. "But any time I come here, I feel as if I'm going back to ancient times."

"That's why a lot of American girls and women are named Candace," said Uncle Leo. "That's where your name came from."

"Well!" said Candace. "You and Anwar may call me 'queen' or the name of a queen, just as long as you treat me like one!"

The two men laughed. "All right, My Lady," Uncle Leo said. "Tomorrow at 6:00 A.M., the queen needs to be up and ready to start work!"

Uncle Leo was an archaeologist. He had led digs all over Africa. He had invited Candace to spend part of her vacation working with him at Meroë [mer'ə•wē'].

"It almost rhymes with 'narrow way,'" she had told her mother. "The kings of Kush ruled there for about 600 years. They were buried in pyramids, like in Egypt."

Uncle Leo had sent Candace a plane ticket to Khartoum, Sudan. There he had met her with his hired truck.

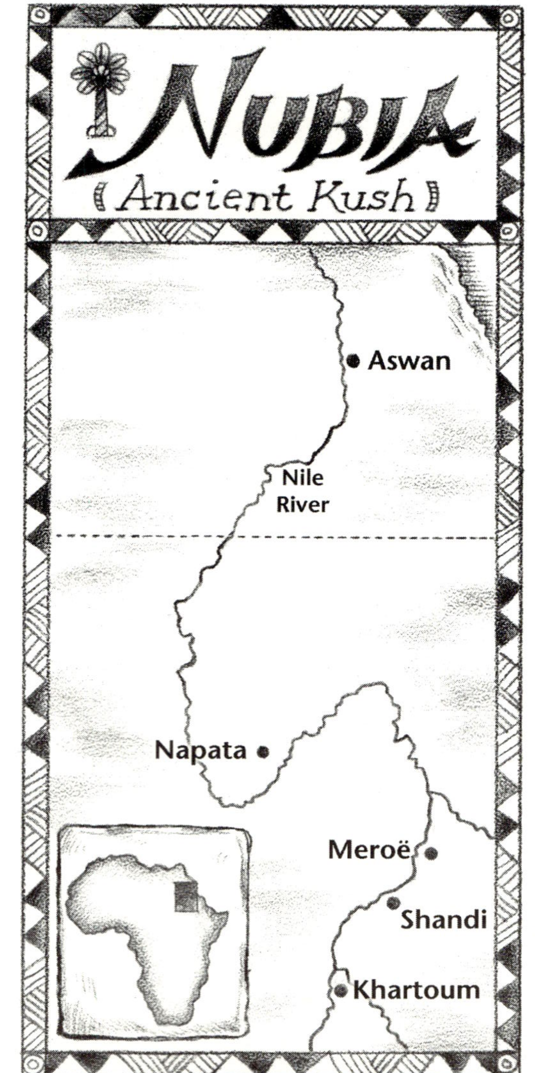

Harcourt

"You see, Kandake—*Candace*," said her uncle, "*Kandake* was the word for 'queen' in the language of Kush. Around 24 B.C. the Roman Empire tried to take over Kush. A queen led the army that stopped their advance. A Roman writer called her Candace in a book he wrote. He didn't know the word meant 'queen.' He thought it was her name."

Harcourt

"Some day," Anwar said, "someone may dig up a stone with a long written passage in both Egyptian and Nubian. Then some ingenious scholar will be able to translate our ancient language. Perhaps it will be you, Kandake."

"Anwar, why do you keep calling me 'con-*dah*-kay'? You know my name is Candace." Candace thought she was being teased.

"Don't you know?" asked Anwar with a grin. "Professor, why don't you tell her?"

"Meroë is pretty isolated now, but once it was the capital of a great kingdom," Uncle Leo said. "The important buildings were made of stone brought there from quarries. Because it's in the desert, it has been well preserved. Many archaeologists have worked there, but there's still a lot to discover."

"We're getting near Shandi," said Anwar, their driver. "Shall we show Kandake the ruins?"

"Sure, why not?" said Uncle Leo.

"Kush was a great trading nation," Uncle Leo explained. "Kushite traders carried gold, ivory, and rare wood to Egypt from other parts of Africa. Later, Greek and Roman traders came here, too. This building looks as if it were put together from parts of Egyptian, Greek, and Roman temples."

"*Was* it a temple?" Candace asked.

"No one knows. An archaelogist called it a kiosk, and that's what everyone calls it."

The next afternoon they reached the site of Meroë. Dozens of pyramids covered the ground. They were steeper than the pyramids of Egypt but not nearly as tall. Not far away was an area marked off by ropes.

"That's our dig," said Uncle Leo. "Meroë is not exactly a new site. But because it's so isolated, it has not been explored nearly as well as sites in Egypt."

Harcourt

Harcourt

That night Candace stayed in a guest house in the market town of Shandi. "The kings of Kush built stone palaces," Candace commented. "Why do the Nubians today build with mud bricks?"

"Because we are not kings, Kandake," Anwar said. "Ordinary people cannot have stones brought here from quarries. It was the same in those times. We build with what we have—good old Nile River mud."

"It makes cool, comfortable houses," Uncle Leo added. "They just don't stay preserved for us archaeologists to find."

8

"This building is like nothing anywhere else in the world," said Uncle Leo. They were looking at a ruin filled with rooms, courtyards, and passageways. Pictures of elephants were carved on the outer wall.

"No one knows what this place was used for," said Uncle Leo. "It may have been a temple or a palace. Or, it may have been a cattle market or a stopping place for travelers. A lot of animal bones have been found here, but no tombs."

Candace stared at the enormous ruin. To her it looked like a royal palace. The entrance ramps looked big enough to have been passageways for elephants.

5

Harcourt

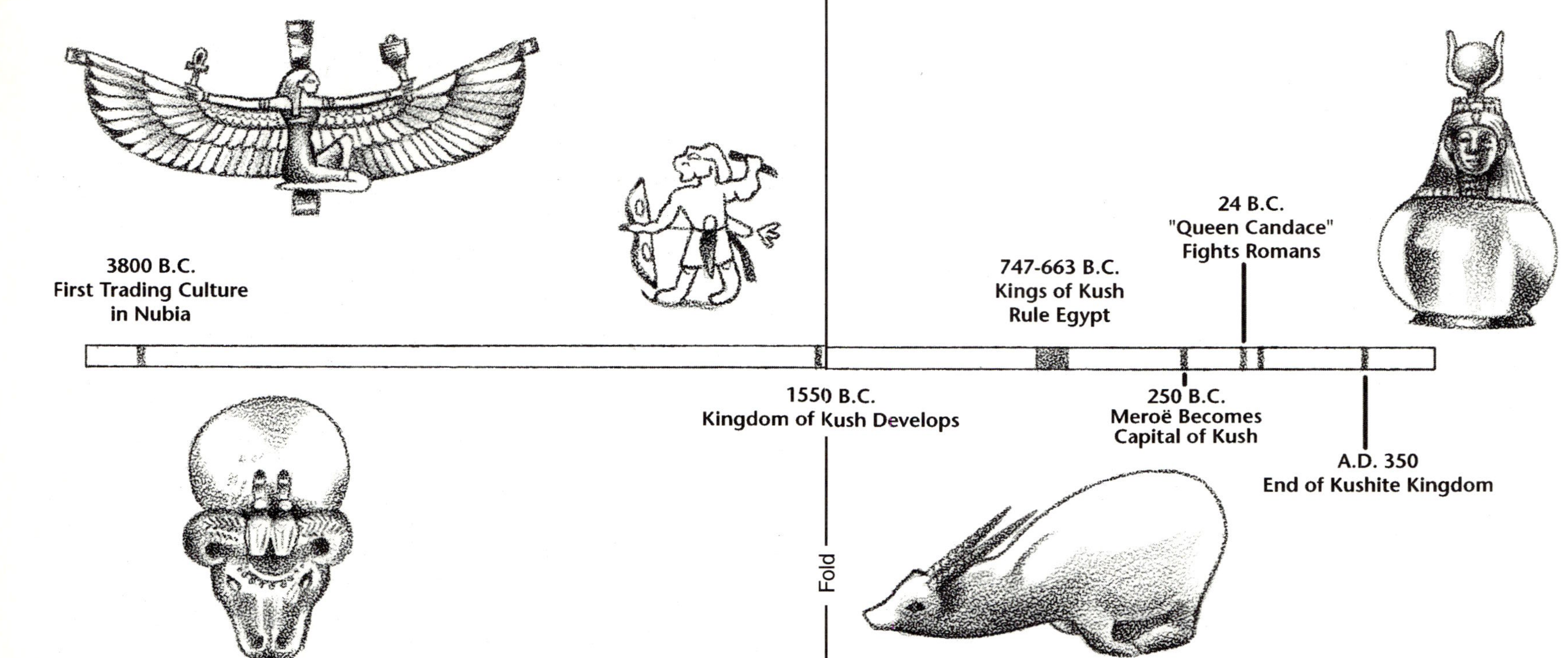

"Uncle Leo," Candace asked, "If Kush was so important, how come so little is known about it?"

"Good question," said her uncle. "It's because no one today can read the Kushitic language. At first, the people of Kush used the Egyptian form of writing. They were often at war with Egypt, but they also borrowed a great deal of their culture from the Egyptians."

"Around 750 B.C., the kings of Kush actually took over Egypt. They ruled as Egypt's twenty-fifth dynasty. But then they were driven back to their capital, Napata. Later they moved the capital farther south to Meroë."

"By then the people of Kush had stopped imitating the Egyptians. Their culture developed in new ways. They invented their own ingenious alphabet. We know how the letters were pronounced, but we don't know what the words mean."

6

7

BLAST FROM THE PAST

by Karen Stamfil

illustrated by Barbara Higgins Bond

— Fold —

Harcourt

TAKE-HOME BOOK
Times of Discovery
Use with "Look Into the Past: The Greeks & Romans."

Answer:

The suspect is Paul. He entered the antiquities shop just as Jason was leaving. There was an artifact in the shop just like the one found in the dig. Paul took the artifact and buried it because he wants scientists to think he's proved the Minoans were here. Then the university would pay for five more years of digging.

Be a Detective

Suppose Jason had to fill out a report about what he suspected. On a sheet of paper, write what he might report. Use the prompts below to get you started. (The answers are on the back of this page.)

I suspect ____.

My reasons are: _______________________________________

____

____

____

____

____

____

____

School-Home Connection Listen as your child reads this book aloud. You and your child may want to visit a museum that displays artifacts from ancient cultures, or look at some together in a library book or on the Internet. Talk about what you see.

Fold

As far as Jason was concerned, *this* was the start of the vacation. For two weeks he and his parents had been seeing the sights of Europe. They had saved and planned for years to make the trip. Now they were in the Greek islands, the place Jason most wanted to visit.

"Look there." Jason's father pointed to a high stone arch. "Is that old enough to make you happy?"

"Not really," Jason said. "It's a Roman aqueduct— probably no more than 2,000 years old."

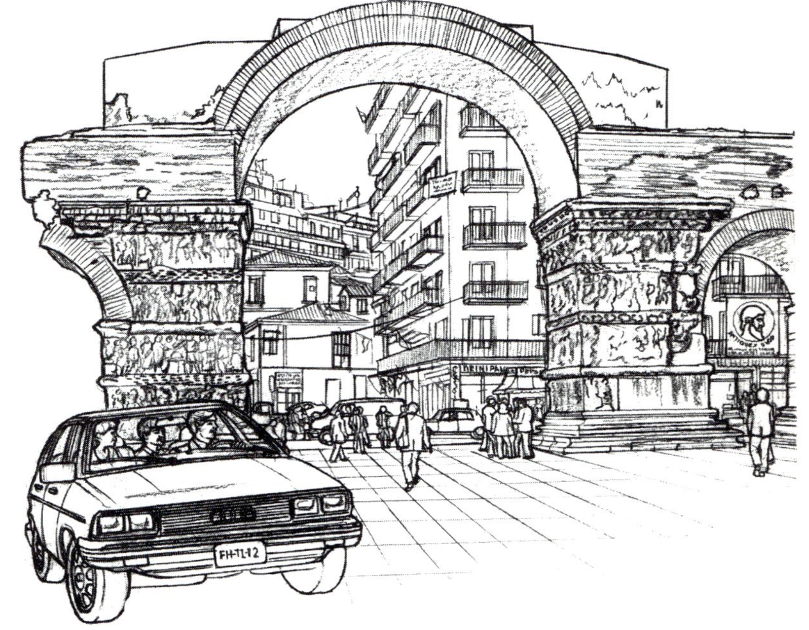

Professor Diaz was still talking to Dr. Pappas. "Excuse me," Jason said. "You may have a problem. Before you make an official report, there are a few things that you may want to check out."

The professor wasn't angry. She said something in Greek to the official. Then Dr. Pappas turned to Jason.

"Dr. Diaz said not to be fooled by how young you are," she said in English. "She says you know a lot about archaeology. So you think you've spotted a fake?"

"Not a fake—a plant," Jason said. "I think someone buried that Minoan artifact there to be found. Here's why. . . ."

Who is the person that Jason suspects? And why does Jason suspect that person?

Harcourt

Jason was delighted to find that there was an archaeological dig not far from their hotel. After lunch he went down there for a look.

The archaeologist in charge was a Professor Diaz, from a university in the United States. She didn't mind Jason's asking her questions.

"You seem to know a lot about ancient Greece," she said. "Yes, we've found some interesting things. This mosaic dates from the third century A.D. Look here. Luke just cleaned the emblem of the artist who made it."

"Anything from classical Greece?" Jason asked.

Jason looked at the sculpture. Why did it look so familiar? He thought about the people he had met at the dig. And he thought about other things he had seen on the island.

"They do have a mystery on their hands!" Jason thought.

Harcourt

Harcourt

Luke showed Jason the artifact. It was a bronze sculpture, still half-buried in sand.

"This is very exciting," Luke said. "You see this image over and over in Minoan art. And it's right at the level where you'd expect to find something Minoan. Sometimes we find an artifact where it has no right to be—like a thousand years too early. Then we have a mystery on our hands."

"Quite a lot," said Professor Diaz. "We've found Athenian coins, household items, and ship hardware. This island was an Athenian colony. The street we're standing on dates from around 450 B.C. The drain in the middle was for public hygiene.

"But we're hoping to find some Minoan artifacts," the professor continued. "My guess is that the Minoans were here, but Luke, Lydia, Paul, and I haven't proved it yet." She smiled. "I hope we do, and soon. Then the university would pay for five more years of digging."

"It would be wonderful to be able to work here for five more years," said Paul.

Harcourt

Later Jason and his parents walked through the town. Jason was still talking about Professor Diaz.

"That would really be something if she found Minoan stuff," he said. "The Minoans lived 3,700 years ago. They built these incredible palaces and created great works of art. They even knew about personal hygiene. They had sewers thousands of years before anyone else."

"Look." Jason's father pointed to a shop near the Roman aqueduct. "Want to have a look?"

All was excitement around the dig. Work seemed to have stopped. Professor Diaz was talking in Greek to a TV reporter. When she recognized Jason, she smiled and waved. Jason waited until the interview was over.

"You brought us good luck!" the professor said. "Lydia here turned up a Minoan artifact this morning. Paul called the Antiquities Ministry in Athens. This is Dr. Pappas. She's an expert the government sends out to the provinces to check on archaeological findings."

"It certainly looks authentic," said Dr. Pappas. "Of course, we can't be sure until we've run some tests."

The next day Jason and his parents took a boat ride around the island. As they cruised back into the harbor, Jason saw activity around the archaeological site.

"That looks like a TV truck," he said.

"And that helicopter has a government emblem," his mother said.

The shop sold antiquities of all kinds. There were tools and pottery, sculpture and writing tablets.

"Do you see anything you like?" the shopkeeper asked in English.

"Not really," Jason said. The only things he could have afforded were some coins with the emblem of the Roman emperor Titus. But he already had enough coins in his collection. "You've got some interesting stuff, though. Is it all from this island?"

Harcourt

Harcourt

"Oh, no," said the shopkeeper. "People bring me things from all over." She pointed to a small pot. "This was found on the island of Kos. And this mosaic is from a Roman estate in Thrace. Or was it Achaea? One of the provinces of their empire."

"That's the trouble with shops like that," Jason thought to himself. "They'll buy and sell anything. They don't care where it comes from, or from when. It's hard to reconstruct the past if you don't leave things in place. That's the only way they can be studied properly."

"Thanks for the information. I guess I should be going," Jason said to the shopkeeper as he walked toward the door.

Just as Jason was leaving, Paul entered the shop and bumped into Jason.

"Oh, excuse me," Jason said. "That's okay." Paul said as he hurried into the store.

"Hmm," Jason thought. "I guess he's in as big a hurry as I am to reconstruct the past."

Harcourt

TAKE-HOME BOOK
Times of Discovery
Use with "The Skill of Pericles."

JUST HOW DEMOCRATIC WAS PERICLES' ATHENS?

by Frank Maltesi
illustrated by Katy Robert

Be an Orator

On a separate sheet of paper, write a short speech to persuade someone to share your opinion about something. Then practice giving your speech.

Fold

School-Home Connection Listen as your child reads this book aloud. Then discuss the differences between the rights of a citizen of Athens and the rights of a citizen of the United States.

Harcourt

The tricky words here are *citizen* and *man*. Only people born to two Athenian parents could be citizens. Pericles himself got this law passed. Perhaps half the people in Athens were not citizens. They did most of the work and ran the day-to-day business in the agora. But they had no voice in the Assembly.

Among the citizens, only men took part in public life. Women were expected to stay at home. Pericles himself said that a woman's greatest honor was "to be least talked about by men."

So, was Athens a democracy, or was it only disguised as one? What do you think?

12

The Parthenon[1] stands on the Acropolis,[2] a hill high above the city of Athens, in Greece. You can see it from miles away as you approach the city. It was the same 2,400 years ago, when the Parthenon was new. A man named Pericles planned it that way.

Pericles, Athens' leading citizen from 460 to 429 B.C., called Athens "an education to Greece." Putting up buildings like the Parthenon was one way he tried to make this boast come true.

[1]**Parthenon** [pär′thə·nän′]

[2]**Acropolis** [ə·krä′pə·ləs]

1

The time of Pericles' influence is sometimes called the Golden Age of Athens because Athens was "an education to Greece"—and to much of the world ever since. Athenian plays from that time are still performed today. Artists today still study and admire Athenian sculpture. In Pericles' day, medicine became a science and history became a search for truth.

This period is also called a Golden Age because Athens was a democracy—the world's first. But was it what we call a democracy today? Was Pericles a wise and skillful ruler chosen by the people? Or was he a tyrant disguised as a democratic leader? Let's take a look.

Harcourt

Early in the war Pericles had persuaded people from the surrounding countryside to move to Athens for safety. The Spartans burned their villages. Disease broke out in the crowded city. Thousands died. The angry Athenians blamed Pericles. He was driven from office and died in 429 B.C.

So—how democratic was Pericles' Athens?

Every citizen could serve in the Assembly and on the Council. Any man might become as powerful as Pericles, if he had his virtues.

Harcourt

The Athenian empire worried other Greek states. They feared that Athens would impose its way on them, too. Many of them looked to Sparta, a state in southern Greece, for help.

Sparta was a powerful state. Athens and Sparta had been allies in the wars against the Persians. But now the two states were looking at each other as enemies. In 431 B.C. war broke out between Athens and Sparta.

The war lasted twenty-seven years and ended in the defeat of Athens. But the Golden Age of Athens had ended long before that.

Under Athens' laws, the Athenian Assembly ruled the state. Every male, free-born citizen of Athens, rich or poor, was a member of the Assembly.

The Assembly met forty times a year. Any member could speak on any subject. But if he simply stood there bellowing his views, no one would listen.

That's why Athenians counted oratory—the art of public speaking—among the greatest virtues. A great orator could rouse the Assembly to agree with him by the power of his words. Pericles was one of the greatest of the orators.

The Assembly met near the agora. On most days this busy marketplace was filled with shopkeepers and customers.

But the agora was also a place for state business. Orators would speak on issues that were before the Assembly, trying to win members' votes.

Pericles won respect for his dignity and wisdom in the agora. Stories tell how he remained calm even when others were bellowing insults at him.

Much of this money came from the Delian League. Its treasury had been kept in the island state of Delos. But in 453 B.C. the Assembly had it moved to Athens. The treasury's money came from all over Greece, but the Athenians were now using it for their own projects.

Athens had become the ruler of an empire. States that tried to leave the Delian League were considered enemies and were attacked by Athens.

Harcourt

Harcourt

Pericles wanted to make Athens' power visible. Many of the city's public buildings had been destroyed during the Persian Wars. The Parthenon was only one of many new buildings that Pericles had ordered to be built. He hired the greatest architects and artists to build and decorate them. He persuaded the Assembly to put up money every year for his building projects.

The Assembly did have a list of matters to discuss at its meetings. The list was prepared by a council of 500 men, called the Boule (bū′lē). Any Assembly member over thirty could volunteer to serve on the Boule. Its members were chosen by lot. They served for a term of one year and could not serve for more than two terms.

It was Pericles who saw to it that members of the Boule were paid. He was rich and could afford to serve on the Boule without pay. This law made it possible for poor men to serve, too.

Harcourt

An Executive Council of fifty men carried out the will of the Assembly. They were chosen from the Boule, and the membership changed every few weeks. Each day a different member served as chairman. This rule was meant to keep anyone from gaining too much power.

In fact, though, the chairman was always one of the ten generals of Athens' army. The generals were chosen by the Assembly. If one was an outstanding leader, he could usually rouse the Assembly to vote his way. During the Golden Age, one man gained such influence—Pericles.

Pericles became powerful by making the city-state of Athens powerful. He sent ships to start new trading colonies. He also formed alliances with other seagoing Greek states. Athens led an alliance of more than 200 states called the Delian League. Each member contributed ships or money for defense against the barbarians.

Today the word *barbarians* means "brutes." To the Greeks it meant "anyone who is not Greek"—especially the Persians. They were hardly brutes, but the Greeks had recently fought two wars against them, and they were still powerful enemies.

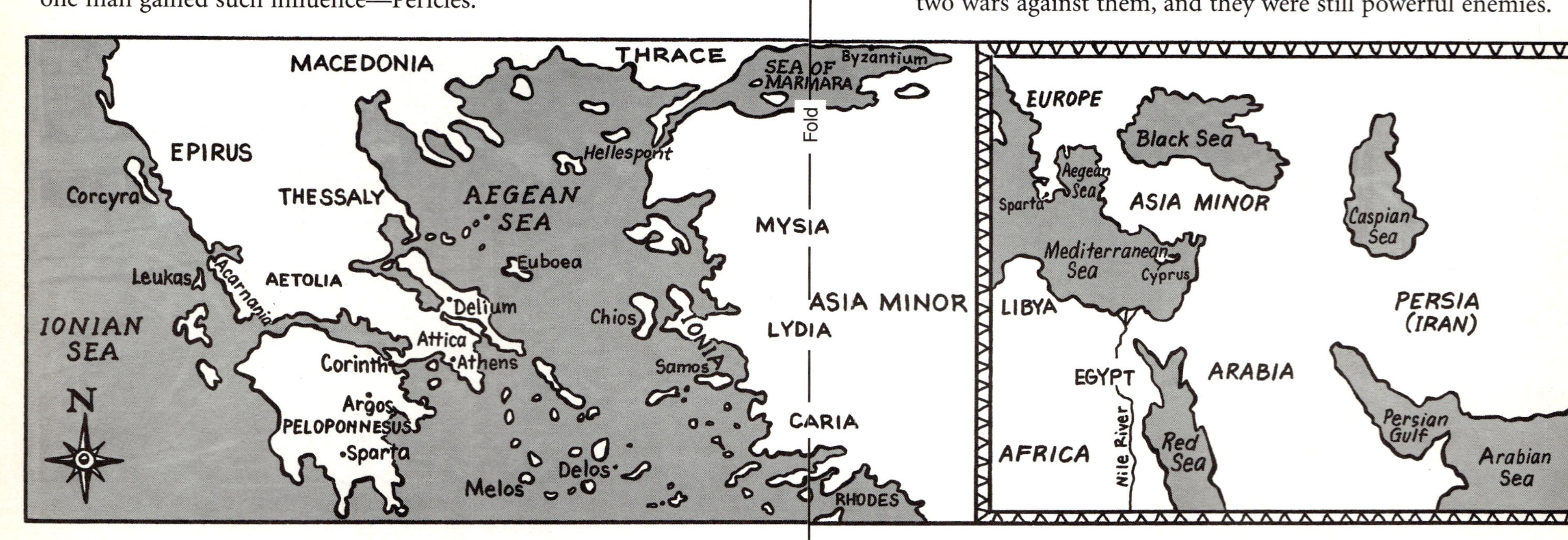

Harcourt

TAKE-HOME BOOK
Times of Discovery
Use with "My Side of the Mountain."

The Crater

by Mark Falstein
illustrated by Steven Francis

Fact and Fiction

The Crater is science fiction. It contains some facts but also some things that were made up for the story. On a separate sheet of paper, make two columns with the headings *Fact* and *Fiction*. In the columns, identify three science facts and three nonfacts in *The Crater.*

Fact   **Fiction**

Fold

School-Home Connection Listen as your child reads this book aloud. Then watch a science fiction movie together. With your child, discuss what is appealing about science fiction stories.

Harcourt

I'm alive. That was Soto's first thought after the crash. He could see the orange glow of the Titan sky. He could hear the *Landcraft 3*'s computer giving a report on the craft's systems.

It was a discouraging report. Forward motion, failed. Lift, failed. Communication, failed. Life support, failing fast. Soto was alive, but his landcraft was dead.

The dust storm had struck suddenly. Before Soto could react, the landcraft had been thrown out of control. He remembered the last thing he had seen. It was a crater, a huge cavity in the rocky surface. His wrecked landcraft now lay at the bottom of that crater.

On the fifth day after leaving the crater, he was rescued. He had never been so glad to see another human being.

"You're looking very fit for someone who's been missing almost a week," Beltran said. "What have you been living on—rocks?"

Soto smiled. There was a lot to tell, but there would be an official report to make first.

"Let me just say this for now," Soto said. "If our food supply at Titan Base ever fails, we won't starve."

Soto checked his space suit. It was not damaged. He climbed out of the landcraft and inflated the portable habitat. Only then did he remove his helmet and begin to consider his problem.

He was in a crater on Titan, the largest moon of Saturn. The crater was in a remote area, far from Titan Base. He had been on a course toward the Great Southern Sea, near the largest of Titan's mysterious "warm spots."

People would come looking for him. But where would they look? The storm had blown him off course. But how far off course? Where was he?

Late on the second day, Soto reached the rim of the crater and climbed out. He was very hungry.

Soto ate some of the Titan moss.

It tasted . . . *brown*. It was not what he would ever choose to eat. But it was edible.

It kept him alive for four days.

Harcourt

Soto slept. The next morning he gathered more of the "Titan moss."

He wondered where the oxygen in this living thing could have come from. Then he considered that Titan had plenty of water in the form of ice. Living things deep in Earth's oceans got oxygen directly from water. Maybe life here had a way of taking it from ice.

He looked at the shadows. Even through thick clouds, the sun was much brighter than the full moon as seen from Earth. And giant Saturn, only 1.2 million kilometers away, gave off its own reflected light.

But the cavity of the crater had steep walls. The wreck was in deep shadow. A rescue party might easily miss sighting him. And radio signals did not work well on Titan. There was too much interference from Saturn.

He realized he had to get out of the crater.

Harcourt

He ate and rested. He could carry the habitat, but food would be a problem if he was not found soon. He had only enough to last two days.

He gazed at the crater's high wall. The view was discouraging. He had climbed steeper rocks on Earth, and at Titan's gravity he was only a fraction of his normal weight. But he had been living at low gravity for two Earth years. How strong was he now?

Harcourt

No, it wasn't a plant. "Plants" grew only on Earth. This was something else. It was not DNA-based life. But it was alive. It was organized in cells. It contained the same elements as life on Earth. If he ate it, his body could break it down for his cells to use. To Soto, as a scientist, that was what "nourishing" meant.

But he didn't eat it. The computer did not indicate any poisons, but why should he experiment on himself? He wasn't starving—yet.

On Earth he would have observed whether animals ate the stuff. That would tell him if it was safe. But there were no animals on Titan—or were there?

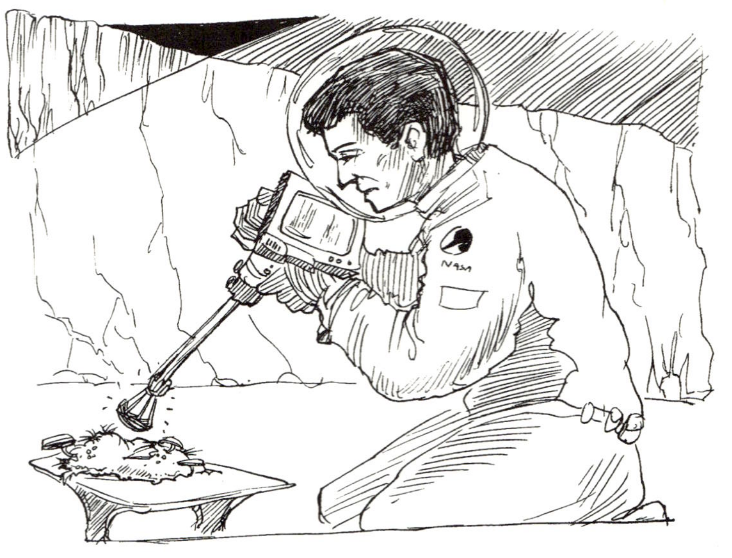

Harcourt

Soto was a pioneer. He and others on this remote moon were preparing the way for a migration. Titan Base would be the foundation of a domed city.

Hydrogen was the reason for the migration. Earth in 2064 ran on hydrogen fusion power. The new fusion spaceships took only months to reach Saturn and only weeks to reach Mars. Saturn was a giant hydrogen mine that would never run out.

But there were other reasons to be here. Ever since the Cassini and Huygens probes of 2004, scientists had wanted to learn more about Titan's warm spots.

Carefully, Soto scraped up some of the soft, dark stuff. It came away from the rock with difficulty. He looked around and found a large, flat rock that could serve as a foundation for his portable habitat.

Inside, he kept his helmet on. He set up the portable lab. He tested a sample of the substance.

It was alive! Not only alive, but edible. Not only edible, but nourishing! It was a living, growing plant.

Titan was a world of rock and ice. The surface temperature was about –180°C. There were no volcanoes. Yet here and there were areas no colder than a winter day on Earth. What were they?

Soto climbed. In some places he had to pull himself up hand over hand. In others he had to leap over deep, wide cracks.

It would soon be night. He had to set up the habitat. It would be dangerous to—

Soto stopped. He checked his space suit's built-in computer. Yes! *Right here* was a warm spot. It was almost warm enough to take off his space suit—if Titan had had any oxygen to breathe.

And what were those dark streaks running along the rock? They looked like orange moss.

Harcourt

Harcourt

TAKE-HOME BOOK
Times of Discovery
Use with "Febold Feboldson."

Answers:
1. Sutter   2. Marshall   3. forty-niners   4. Oregon   5. California   6. law
7. diggings   8. San Francisco   9. out   10. Strauss   11. rich

12. Hidden message: **the gold rush**

The California Gold Rush

by Meish Goldish
illustrated by Ken Bowser

Find the Hidden Message

On a separate sheet of paper, write the answer to each clue. Then use the hidden message in the boxes to answer question 12. It tells you what happened in 1849. (The answers are on the next page.)

1. Gold was found at his mill.   ___ ___ ☐ ___ ___ ___

2. He found the gold first.   ___ ___ ___ ___ ☐ ___ ___ ___

3. What gold seekers were called
    ___ ___ ___ ___ ___-___ ___ ___ ☐ ___ ___

4. Trail many took to California   ___ ___ ___ ☐ ___ ___

5. It became a state in 1850.
    ___ ___ ___ ___ ___ ☐ ___ ___ ___ ___

6. What sheriffs tried to uphold   ☐ ___ ___

7. Another name for miners' camps ☐ ___ ___ ___ ___ ___ ___ ___

8. This port town grew rapidly.
    ___ ___ ___ ___ ☐ ___ ___ ___ ___ ___ ___

9. To "pan ___" (an expression)   ___ ☐ ___

10. He invented tough jeans.   ☐ ___ ___ ___ ___ ___

Hidden Message:

11. What gold seekers wanted to become   ___ ___ ___ ☐

12. ___ ___ ___   ___ ___ ___ ___   ___ ___ ___ ___

School-Home Connection Listen as your child reads this book aloud. Then talk with him or her about ways in which life in 1849 was different from life today. What inventions now exist that didn't exist back then?

Harcourt

Within a decade the California gold rush had vaporized into cloudy memories, but the effects of this great event were far-reaching and powerful. After the gold rush ended, many people continued to move to California. Cities such as San Francisco and Sacramento became major industrial centers. Farming and ranching also expanded across the state.

It had all begun with the discovery of a few precious gold nuggets at Sutter's Mill. In the end the gold rush helped develop the entire state of California and the western United States.

"I found gold! I found gold!"

Those are the words that James Marshall most likely shouted after discovering a few nuggets of the precious

ore in California in 1848. Marshall, a carpenter, had been hired by John Sutter to build a sawmill along the American River, about 100 miles from San Francisco.

On January 24, 1848, while busy at work, Marshall happened to find gold in the river at Sutter's Mill. The news of his discovery spread slowly at first, since telephones had not yet been invented. But over time thousands of people heard the news and raced to the area to seek gold for themselves. By 1849, California's gold rush was in full swing.

The gold seekers, known as "forty-niners," came to California from all parts of the world. The first forty-niners arrived in San Francisco by ship on February 28, 1849. Soon after, more ships brought thousands of others.

Most Americans heading for California went by covered wagon along the Oregon Trail. The trip took months and was hard and dangerous. Families had to race against time to avoid being stranded by winter snow. Along the way some travelers clashed with Native Americans who felt threatened by strangers on their land.

One day Strauss approached a miner and asked if he wanted to buy canvas for a tent. (Canvas is a very strong cloth that is difficult to tear.)

The miner replied that he already had a tent but needed sturdier pants. Because the miner worked on his hands and knees all day, his pants and pockets ripped easily.

Strauss suddenly got the idea to make pants from his tent canvas. His idea succeeded, and soon thousands of other miners were demanding "those pants of Levi's." As a result, Levi's jeans were born, and Strauss became a very rich merchant.

Harcourt

One person who got rich in the gold rush had not even been seeking gold. Levi Strauss was a businessperson who had moved from New York to California to sell goods to the forty-niners.

Each day Strauss went into the camps with items such as pans, cups, plates, blankets, and tent material. Traveling about the region, he made a decent living selling his wares. Then good fortune wafted his way and changed his life.

For Americans in the East, getting to California was an especially difficult procedure. At the time, railroad tracks did not run from coast to coast as they do today.

Many Easterners first rode trains to the Mississippi River and then completed their trip by covered wagon. Some wagons did not survive the steep mountains, and people had to walk long distances.

Other travelers took a ship to Panama, walked to the Pacific Ocean, and then took a second ship to California.

Still other voyagers sailed around the tip of South America and up the California coast.

Harcourt

Despite the hardships of travel, people eagerly poured into California. In just one year San Francisco grew from a small port town to a major city. New stores and hotels sprang up each week. Sacramento, another small town at the time, also grew rapidly.

By 1850, California had enough residents to become the newest state in the United States. During the next ten years, the state's population expanded from 26,000 to 380,000.

4

Sadly, most forty-niners found little or no gold at all. After months or years of failure, their hopes of striking it rich vaporized. Their dreams of success did not "pan out" (an expression referring to the pan that miners used to separate the gold from the other materials).

No longer intrigued by gold, some forty-niners made the long journey back home. But many others stayed in California and became farmers and ranchers in the Sacramento Valley.

9

Harcourt

Forty-niners who found gold usually returned to town to spend part or all of their new wealth. Businesses grew rapidly as a result.

New neighborhoods sprang up, also. Many a miner replaced his shanty with a larger, more comfortable home.

Unfortunately, the increase in wealth also brought an increase in crime. Thieves often stole gold from miners in the camps. Some miners were killed for their gold. Sheriffs did their best to protect citizens, but keeping law and order in the "Wild West" was often a difficult task.

Everyone was intrigued by the possibility of striking it rich. There were stories about gold miners who became millionaires overnight. Many a poor family dreamed of finding gold, moving out of their shanty, and building a large, modern home.

Yet few of the forty-niners actually became wealthy. There was gold in California, but not enough to make everybody rich. In fact, most miners got little or nothing for their efforts. A full week of mining often resulted in no gold at all.

Most forty-niners set up camps, or "diggings," where they worked alone or with partners to search for gold. During meal breaks, the smell of hot coffee and fried food wafted through the air.

Some miners worked in the camps five days a week, returning to their wives and children in town only on weekends. Other miners, especially those without families, stayed at the diggings full-time, looking for gold.

Hunting for the yellow metal was not an easy procedure. Diggers worked on their hands and knees all day, "panning" for gold. They swirled water and gravel around in an ordinary frying pan. The smaller, lighter particles washed out of the pan, leaving the heavier gold bits inside.

Other miners used a shovel to scoop gravel into a container with a screen on the bottom. Then they rocked the container back and forth, sifting out other material until only the gold remained.

Harcourt

6

7

Harcourt

TAKE-HOME BOOK
Times of Discovery
Use with "The Kid Who Invented the Popsicle."

The "Mother" of Invention

by David Galash
illustrated by Mary Ball

Your Own Invention

What do you think would be a useful invention? On a separate sheet of paper, draw a picture of what it might look like. Then write a short explanation of how it works.

Fold

School-Home Connection Listen as your child reads this book aloud. Then walk around in your home and point out inventions that didn't exist when you were a child or that existed in a very different form.

Harcourt

Josephine Garis Cochrane's patent was sold to an Ohio company. It became a leading maker of home appliances. And in the 1950s, dishwashing machines finally caught on.

By then their inventor was all but forgotten. Even in Shelbyville, Illinois, few people knew that a much-used invention had originated in their town.

Finally, in 1993, Josephine Garis Cochrane was honored with a monument. It stands in front of the house where she built her first dishwasher more than a hundred years ago.

12

Josephine Garis Cochrane didn't wash dishes. She didn't have to. She was a wealthy widow, and her servants did that job. The problem was that they weren't doing it very well. From this problem came an opportunity.

Mrs. Cochrane often gave dinner parties at her home in Shelbyville, Illinois. It seemed that every time she did, the servants broke some of her expensive dishes. This was during the 1880s. It took months to get the dishes replaced by mail.

It was a great age of invention. The telephone, lightbulb, refrigerator, and electric fan all had appeared in the last few years. Why, Mrs. Cochrane wondered, had no one invented a machine for washing dishes?

Finally she declared, "If no one else is going to invent a dishwashing machine, I'll do it myself!"

1

Harcourt

Josephine Garis was born in Ohio in 1839 and grew up in small towns in the Midwest. Invention ran in her family. Her father designed bridges and machines. Her great-grandfather was John Fitch, who built the first successful steamboat in 1786.

At the age of nineteen, Garis married William Cochrane, a politician from Shelbyville. It was soon after his death in 1883 that the idea of a dishwashing machine originated in her mind.

2

Some American women at the time *liked* doing dishes. They found it relaxing. They would welcome other laborsaving machines, such as one for washing clothes. But a dishwasher just wasn't considered essential.

The company tried another approach. A machine could use much hotter water than human hands could stand. Dishwashers not only got dishes cleaner but also killed more germs.

The machine still would not sell.

11

Harcourt

Mrs. Cochrane kept improving her home machine, but hotels and restaurants remained her best customers.

Josephine Garis Cochrane died in Chicago in 1913. She remained active in her business until the last year of her life.

A year after her death, her company came out with a new home dishwasher. It too was a failure.

Company managers wanted to find out why. They discovered an amazing fact that Josephine Cochrane had never realized.

Mrs. Cochrane set up a workshop in a shed behind her home. She hired a young railroad mechanic, George Butters, to help her build the machine, but the design was all her own.

The body of the machine was a large copper boiler. A wheel was fitted into the center. Mrs. Cochrane measured her dishes. She made wire compartments to hold the dishes and fitted them around the edge of the wheel.

A hand pump forced hot, soapy water up through the boiler. The water rained down on the dishes as the wheel turned. Mrs. Cochrane then poured boiling water from a teakettle to rinse the dishes. She let them dry in the air.

Harcourt

It was quite a gimmick, and it worked. Mrs. Cochrane gave a demonstration for her friends. They were impressed. Some asked her to build copies of the machine for them.

Mrs. Cochrane kept improving her design. Word began to get around. When orders started coming in from hotels and restaurants, Mrs. Cochrane knew she had more than a novelty on her hands. She got a patent on her machine in 1886.

At $350, the home dishwashing machine was a very expensive novelty. A few well-to-do people bought the machines, but they were priced too high for most American homes. For many working families at the time, $350 represented almost a year's pay.

In addition, running the machine took more hot water than most homes had available. And in many places, the water was "hard." It contained minerals that made it difficult to get dishes clean without scrubbing.

Harcourt

By 1898 Mrs. Cochrane had built her own factory. Still with her as factory manager was George Butters.

Mrs. Cochrane's machines had become essential to many restaurant and hotel managers. The largest model cleaned, rinsed, and dried up to twenty dozen pieces in just a few minutes. It sold for $1,000. A smaller model held five dozen pieces. It was priced at $700.

Now Mrs. Cochrane had something new in mind. She wanted to build a still smaller dishwasher for private homes. In 1905 the Garis-Cochrane Domestic Dishwashing Machine went on the market. It was a beauty. It was a failure.

The "Garis-Cochrane Dishwashing Machine" made news in the restaurant and hotel business. One manager declared that it saved him $60 per month on dishes that were no longer being broken.

Mrs. Cochrane realized that she could no longer run her operation from a small-town workshop. In 1891 she moved to Chicago. She found a factory where her machines could be built. She sold stock to finance her business. At first she wanted to offer shares only to women investors, but this plan didn't work out.

In moving to Chicago, Mrs. Cochrane had more in mind than the opportunity offered by a big city. A huge world's fair opened in Chicago in May 1893. All of the nine restaurants at the fair bought her machines. The machines washed 50,000 dishes a day.

One building at the fair featured a demonstration of new inventions. Mrs. Cochrane was the only woman represented among the inventors.

By now her machine had been greatly improved from the gimmick she had fashioned in Shelbyville. It stood eight feet high, eight feet long, and six feet wide. It was powered by a steam engine instead of a hand pump. Dishes were set in wooden baskets that slid in and out. They turned as hot water under pressure rained down on them. Mrs. Cochrane's dishwasher won a prize at the fair.

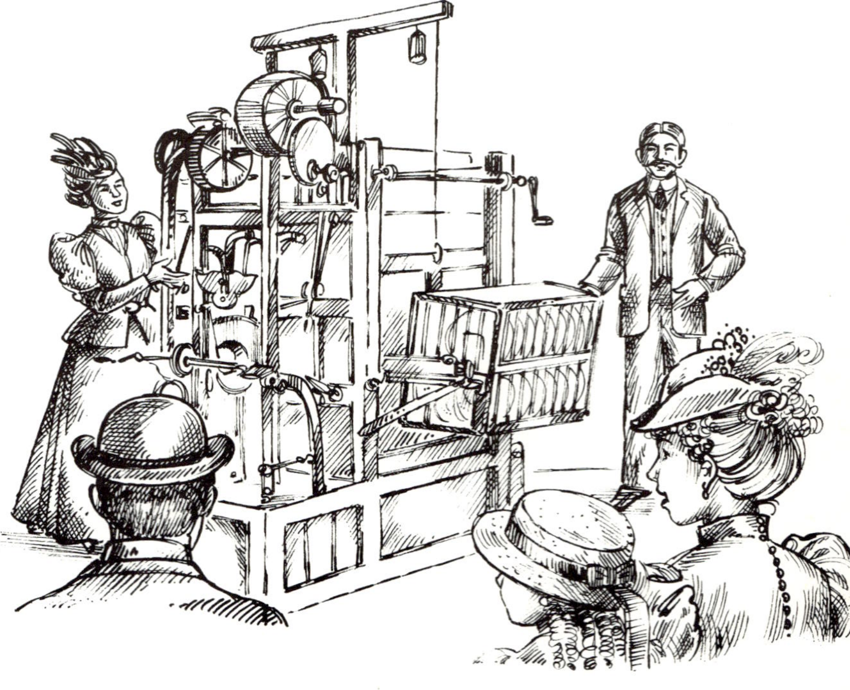

Harcourt

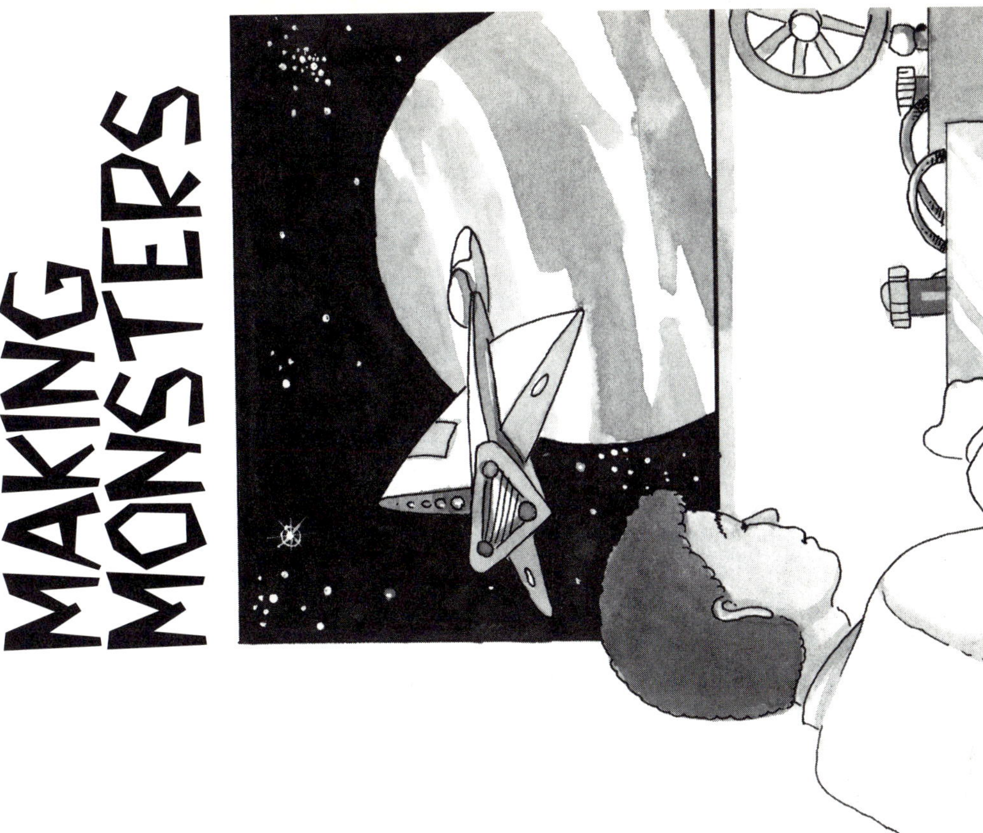

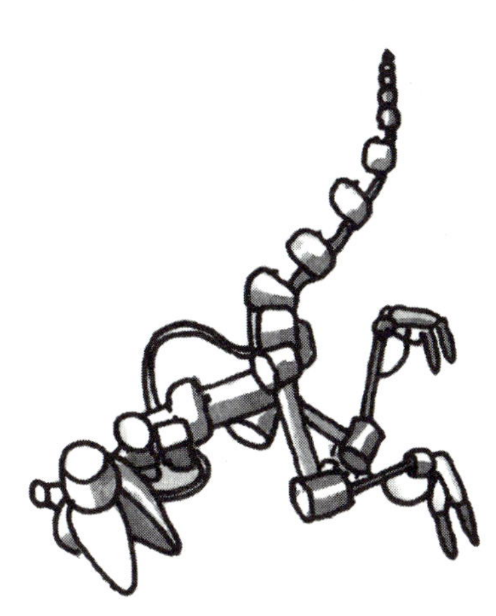

Harcourt

TAKE-HOME BOOK
Times of Discovery
Use with "A Do-It-Yourself Project."

Fold

MAKING MONSTERS

by Isabel Gallego
illustrated by Franklin Ayers

A Day in the Monster Lab

On a separate sheet of paper, write a journal entry for a movie special-effects artist. Describe the work that the artist did on a particular day.

School-Home Connection Listen as your child reads this book aloud. Then talk about a favorite special effect in a movie you have seen together. How do you and your child think the effect was created?

Fold

Harcourt

Of course, computers can do nothing without the work of human brains and hands. But few special-effects artists get special recognition for their work.

So the next time you see a science fiction movie, stick around for the credits. Notice how many names are listed under special effects. Think of all the planning, imagination, and hard work it takes to create a few moments of movie fun.

A Tyrannosaurus rex rises menacingly above the trees. It looks so realistic that you can almost believe it's an actual dinosaur. It's only after the movie is over that you may ask yourself, "How did they *do* that?"

"They" are movie special-effects artists. Special effects are camera shots that create illusions on film. They can be used to create images of things that cannot be real, such as living dinosaurs. But they are also used when a live shot would be too dangerous or expensive.

Take car crashes, for example. On the screen we see a car full of scared people. In the next instant we see them tossed about as the car rolls over a cliff.

In the first shot we were watching actors in a studio. In the second we were watching a miniature car, a model. The people were puppets. Film editing and our recognition of the car created the effect.

Computer graphics are used to design models. They allow artists to create images in two and three dimensions. They are even used to "clean up" live-action shots. The illusion of flying is still created the old-fashioned way, with wires and props. In the old days, these had to be removed from each frame by hand. Computers now do the job with just a few clicks.

Harcourt

Computer graphics have changed special effects in many ways. In one popular movie of 1989, audiences saw a character age hundreds of years in a few seconds. This was an early example of morphing.

"Morphing" means using a computer to change the shape of an image. The image on film is scanned into the computer. An artist uses a software program to change its shape, frame by frame. The images are then scanned back onto film. The result can look scary—or funny.

A more complicated effect might be used for a forest fire on a hillside. The "forest" is a few Christmas trees. The "hillside" is made of wood, wire, and pipe, painted and covered with foil and dirt. What is actually burning is gas, coming from pipes hidden in the ground. Turn off the gas, and there is no more fire.

The effect is dependent on our imagination. The shot is on the screen for only a few seconds, and we're probably watching the actors, not the scenery.

Special effects start with a team of designers and artists. They study the script of the movie and note every camera shot that will need a special effect. The team members design and draw pictures called storyboards to represent each effect. Some science fiction movies require more than a thousand storyboards.

A camera once had to be held still when filming a moving figure against a matte, or the breaks could be seen between the live and painted images. Then, in the 1970s, a computer-controlled camera called an optical printer made it possible to combine hundreds of moving elements into one smooth image.

By 1994 an even newer process had replaced the optical printer. Live action and background images are scanned into a computer. An artist uses the computer to match the colors and backgrounds. The combined image is then scanned back onto film.

Harcourt

Harcourt

Changing camera speeds is one of the oldest ways of creating special effects. Using matte paintings is another.

A matte is a mask that partly covers film as it moves through the camera. This makes the covered part look black. The space is then filled with a painted image. We might see actors moving across a desert toward a painted city, a spaceship orbiting a painted planet, or waves breaking on a painted island.

The painted matte must blend perfectly with the live action on the film. Otherwise we see lines where the edges meet or colors that don't match.

Next, the team members decide how they are going to create each effect. A monster might be an actor in a costume, a puppet animated by electronics, or a three-dimensional image made on a computer. The choice is dependent on cost, safety, and what will make the effect look most real.

Two or more methods may be used to represent the same effect. That T. Rex might be a miniature in one scene and a computer image in the next.

A three-dimensional model can have many moving parts. Even so, its motion might look fake in an ordinary film shot. To make it look more realistic, special-effects artists use stop-action photography.

Most movie cameras run at a speed of twenty-four pictures, or *frames*, per second. At this speed, most action looks like continuous motion. In stop-action photography, the camera takes one picture at a time. Workers adjust the model slightly after each shot.

Since twenty-four adjustments are needed for every second of movie time, this process is slow. But when the film is run at normal speed, the model appears to move.

Changing camera speeds is a method used for other types of effects too. A photographer may walk along a street taking one picture per second. When the film is run at normal speed, we see a thrilling high-speed chase.

Harcourt

Harcourt

TAKE-HOME BOOK
Times of Discovery
Use with "Catching the Fire: Philip Simmons, Blacksmith."

Answers:
1. bellows   2. tongs   3. anvil   4. forge

Forging Ahead

by Joseph Lehmann
illustrated by B. Walker

Blacksmith Talk

Every art or craft has tools and materials with special names. Some blacksmithing terms are used in this story. On a separate sheet of paper, write the numbers 1–4. Next to each number, write the word from the list below that describes the picture with that number. The answers are on the back of this page.

anvil   bellows   forge   tongs

1. __________

2. __________

3. __________

4. __________

School-Home Connection Listen as your child reads this book aloud. Then go around your home and together identify all the items that could have been made by a blacksmith.

Fold

Harcourt

Did the village blacksmith think of himself as an artist?
Probably not. His was a much-needed and valued
trade. "Art" was something for museums, wealthy
customers, and spare time.

But when you add imagination to skill, art is what you
often get. We see it in the work of master smiths of
earlier times. We see it too in the work of today's
blacksmiths who are learning from the masters' work.

The scene is a large city park. A line of children forms
outside a booth at a summer fair. Other booths feature
food, games, performers, or arts and crafts. None has a
line as long as the one at Chris McFee's booth.

Chris is demonstrating the art of blacksmithing. In his
booth is a portable forge. He holds a small iron rod in
the fire with a pair of tongs while a girl pumps a bellows.
Then he helps a boy beat the rod on an anvil with a
hammer. Sparks fly. The metal hisses as McFee plunges
it into cold water. The rod is now a nail—made the
old way.

Chris McFee gives his demonstrations for fun and education. He is quick to tell you that he isn't really a blacksmith. He is an ornamental woodworker and carpenter in Langley, Washington. "About twenty years ago," he says, "I had this idea about independence. I decided I wanted to make my own tools."

Until about 1900 most iron tools and hardware items were made by hand. There were blacksmiths in every American town and village. (Think of how many people are named Smith!)

Blacksmiths were rugged men with strong arms and hands made hard by work. Their craft was highly respected. Henry Wadsworth Longfellow's poem "The Village Blacksmith" is one of many tributes to their skill.

Younger blacksmiths today think of themselves as artists. Some have even been to art school. Many are members of the ABANA—the Artist-Blacksmith's Association of North America. This group was started in 1973. In that year some young people met in Lumpkin, Georgia, to learn some tips from older smiths. There were twenty-seven people at that first meeting. Today the ABANA has thousands of members.

Harcourt

Harcourt

There is more to blacksmithing than beating hot iron with a hammer. Blacksmithing takes exact timing and a careful set of steps. One wrong blow can ruin hours of work.

Blacksmiths must be able to tell how hot the metal is just by looking at it. They must know when and where to strike. They must understand different kinds of iron and steel and the materials that are mixed with them. They must know how the heated metal will behave when hammered.

Then it became easier for Americans to get factory-made hardware. It was cheaper than handmade products. There was no longer much need for horse-shoes or wagon fittings. Ornamental iron fell out of fashion as a building material.

By 1940 few smiths were still working at their craft. "The village blacksmith" had passed into history.

During the 1960s some Americans became interested
in blacksmithing as an art or hobby. They would install
a forge in a garage and try to make simple tools. The
problem was in finding people who could teach them.

Chris McFee was lucky to live where he did. In small
towns in the West and South, blacksmithing had never
quite died out. There were old smiths who could teach
new ones, as in the old days. A group called the
NorthWest Blacksmith Association was formed to help
support the blacksmiths' craft.

Today Baldwin is known for his handcrafted knives.
Tributes to his work come in from around the world.
Baldwin also teaches a course for beginners at the
Penland School of Crafts in North Carolina. In two weeks
his students learn to make all the basic hand tools that
blacksmiths use.

That doesn't make them blacksmiths, however. In
earlier days a smith spent three to seven years learning
the craft. After eight to ten more years of work, he
could call himself a "master blacksmith."

Harcourt

Harcourt

Phill Baldwin was fascinated by his introduction to the blacksmith's craft. As a child he saw a demonstration much like Chris McFee's. Later he found an old forge at his school. He talked a teacher into letting him try it out.

Baldwin went on to build his own forge and install it in a New York City junk shop. He spent ten years learning to be a blacksmith by trial and error.

8

Tamar Kaufman was not so lucky. She grew up in Brooklyn, New York. She came to blacksmithing through her love of horses, but she couldn't learn the skill in New York City.

Kaufman went to a school for blacksmiths in Oklahoma. Then, with a friend, she started a business called Horseshoeing with a Woman's Touch. They traveled up and down the East Coast, carrying a portable blacksmith's shop in a pickup truck.

5

Making horseshoes is what most city people today think a blacksmith does. In fact, according to some smiths, horseshoeing isn't blacksmithing at all. People who do what Tamar Kaufman does are called farriers.

When people see a blacksmith at work, they are often surprised at the variety in the products of this rugged craft.

Blacksmiths today make handsome handcrafted tools. They make elegant furniture and household items. They make toys and jewelry. They make decorative iron gates for homes, and they make steel sculptures to stand in front of office buildings.

Harcourt

6

7

Harcourt

TAKE-HOME BOOK
Times of Discovery
Use with "Seventh Grade."

Bus Stop

A Play in One Scene

Characters

GWEN   SKIP

JACKY   DELIA

by Mark Falstein
illustrated by Franklin Ayers

Summer Vacation

Choose any of the four characters. On a separate sheet of paper, write a paragraph on how that character may have wished to spend his or her summer vacation.

Fold

School-Home Connection Listen as your child reads this book aloud. Then talk with you child about which character was his or her favorite and why.

Harcourt

GWEN: You know, I was sitting there reading my book, and
  you know what I was thinking? Some teacher today is
  going to ask me to write "How I Spent My Summer
  Vacation." (*To* SKIP) "New school, new world," right? But
  the same old stuff!

JACKY: You know what would be cool? If the teacher had
  us write "How I *Wish* I Had Spent My Summer Vacation!"
  (*They laugh.*)

GWEN: Oh, here's the bus!

(*During the following dialogue, all stand, gather their things,
  and form a line. Lights begin to fade.*)

SKIP: Hey, Delia. Welcome to the neighborhood.

DELIA: Thank you. It's great to meet
  you all.

GWEN: And I do want you to tell me all
  about Italy!

(*Sound of a bus
  approaching.
  The curtain
  falls.*)

12

SETTING: *A sidewalk and curb, seen from the near edge of
  the street. Apartment building in background. A bus stop
  and bench stand at center, a fire hydrant at right. Now
  and then we hear the sound of passing cars.*

AT RISE: GWEN *is sitting on the bench, reading a book, a
  backpack at her feet.* JACKY *enters left. He is riding a
  skateboard. He jumps off the board, flipping and catching
  it. He looks uncertainly at* GWEN. *Did she see his trick or
  not? She glances at him and sees him watching her. She
  nervously starts to thrust her book into her backpack.
  Then she changes her mind and goes back to her reading,
  holding the book close to her face.*

1

JACKY (*Stepping off of his skateboard*): Hi.

GWEN (*Not looking up*): Hi.

(JACKY, *trying to appear casual, crosses in front of* GWEN *and sits to her left. He peers at the cover of her book, but* GWEN *holds it against her body.*)

GWEN (*Annoyed*): Do you mind?

JACKY: Hey, I only wanted to see what you're reading.

GWEN: Jacky, I realize this is a public bus stop, but that doesn't give you the right to invade my privacy.

JACKY (*Backing off quickly*): Well, excuse me! What's the big deal? Everyone reads that Scared Stiff series. It's really cool.

GWEN (*Returning to her book*): Yes, isn't it?

SKIP (*Sheepishly*): Well, it's not exactly a band yet.

DELIA: I understand. You're just getting started.

SKIP (*With a look at* JACKY): Well, I wouldn't exactly say that, either. Right now, it's more like an idea. (*With a flourish*) But if we have the conviction, we'll be propelled to the top of the charts on a beam of light!

(SKIP *laughs.* DELIA *joins in but is clearly embarrassed.*)

DELIA: I guess sometimes I express myself too strongly.

GWEN: I guess sometimes we all do. (*They all look at her.*) I'm sorry, Skip. You too, Jacky. Sorry about how I talked to you.

JACKY (*After a pause*): It's cool, Gwen.

SKIP: Forget it, Gwen.

Harcourt

Harcourt

DELIA (*Breaking the silence*): Skip, I heard you said that drama is an elective at Woodside?

SKIP: Yeah.

DELIA: Do they do real plays, or do they just, you know, do kid things?

SKIP (*Looking at her*): My sister was in *Romeo and Juliet* there last year. That real enough for you?

DELIA: That's fine. That's wonderful. I didn't mean to insult your school—our school. I just want to be in a program that will let me express myself. Tell me something about yourself, Skip. Tell me about this band you're in—the Sleepless Knights. Could I come hear you play some time?

(JACKY *throws a scowl at her.* SKIP *enters right. At the same time,* DELIA *enters right.* SKIP *taps* JACKY *on the shoulder.* JACKY *looks up, startled.* GWEN *again clutches her book and then relaxes as the two boys greet each other.*)

JACKY: Hey, Skipster!

SKIP: Hey, Jacky! Where have you been all summer?

(SKIP *comes around the right side of the bench. He and* JACKY *give each other "high fives." During the following dialogue,* DELIA *first looks at the boys uncertainly but then comes over to sit on the bench next to* GWEN. *This forces* GWEN *reluctantly closer to* JACKY.)

JACKY: Oh, you know. Riding my board. Mostly I bustled
   around making deliveries for my mom's store. You?
SKIP: Oh, you know, stuff. Swimming. Tennis. Practicing
   with my band.
JACKY: You're in a band?
SKIP: Oh, didn't you know? "The Sleepless Knights." Get it?
   Knights? Like in chess?
JACKY: Cool. What kind of music do you play?
SKIP (*Evasively*): Oh, you know. Rock and roll, a little
   country. (*He plays an imaginary guitar.*)
JACKY: Hey, I didn't know you played guitar. Is music going
   to be your elective at Woodside?

Harcourt

GWEN: Well, an airplane's safer. What's your name?
DELIA: Delia. (*She nods to the boys.* JACKY, *flustered,
   takes out his skateboard and begins rocking.*)
GWEN: Where in Italy do you live?
DELIA: My dad lives in Rome, but he travels a lot on
   business. Siena, Milan—he and I have bustled all over.
SKIP: Hey, we studied ancient Rome last year.
GWEN: Skip, she doesn't care!
SKIP: Hey, what's got into you? (*Handing her the book with
   a scowl*) Here. Have a nice trip.
(*He turns away.* GWEN *stares at the book, looks at* SKIP,
   and then slowly returns the book to her backpack.)

Harcourt

DELIA: Every summer since I was six. My dad lives there.

JACKY: Cool. And your mom lives here?

DELIA: No, my grandmother. (*For a moment, she loses her air of cool serenity, but she quickly recovers.*) Italy is marvelous, Gwen. If it's your conviction that you belong there, I'm sure you'll be propelled to Italy on a beam of light!

(*The others look at* DELIA *strangely for a moment.*)

SKIP: I don't know. Maybe. What's an elective? (JACKY *looks at him in disbelief.* SKIP *laughs.*) Just kidding. I haven't decided. Music, drama, wood shop, Chinese. New school, new world, know what I mean? (*He turns to the girls.*) Hi, Gwen.

GWEN (*Looks up briefly and smiles*): Hi.

JACKY: Watch it, Skip, you're invading her privacy. (*He offers* GWEN *another scowl.*) As if I haven't known her since kindergarten or anything.

GWEN (*Under her breath*): Some boys act like they're still *in* kindergarten.

JACKY: Who, me?

GWEN: I wasn't talking to you!

SKIP: Whoa, did I miss something here?

JACKY: Ask her!

SKIP (*Sitting down between* GWEN *and* JACKY): This is Gwen Barnes, right? Ms. Let's-Have-a-Party? The quickest point guard in the sixth grade?

GWEN (*Quietly*): We're not in sixth grade any more.

SKIP: Really? So how did you spend your summer vacation? Deciding to dump on all your friends so you could make all new ones?

GWEN: I spent it putting aside childish things! (*She tries again to put the book in her backpack. Another book inside the backpack falls out onto the street. She lunges for it, but* SKIP *reaches it first. He looks at the cover.*)

SKIP: *Travels in Italy*?

GWEN (*Sheepishly*): Will you give me my book, please?

SKIP (*Opening the book*): "Museums and galleries of Florence?" "Where to stay in Venice?" Your family's going to Italy?

GWEN: Yes! I mean, no! I'm just reading about it. Is that a problem for you, Mr. Rock-and-Roll Star?

DELIA: Italy is lovely, Gwen. I hope you do get there. (*Everyone turns and looks at* DELIA.)

GWEN: You've been to Italy?

Harcourt

TAKE-HOME BOOK
Times of Discovery
Use with "Fall Secrets."

Fold

Mine for a Song

by Karen Stamfil
illustrated by C. Matthew Slade

Design a CD Cover

What kind of music would Yvonne sing if she had her chance?
On a separate sheet of paper, draw the cover for a CD she
might record.

Fold

School-Home Connection Listen as your child reads this book aloud. Then talk with your child about the musical terms and expressions used in the story. Together, look up the meanings of those you or your child don't understand.

Yvonne Ortiz saw the poster on a bulletin board. "YOURS FOR A SONG," it said. "Join the school chorus. Sign up here for auditions." At the bottom it said, "Mr. Yesler, Director, Room 107."

That's for me, Yvonne thought. She put her name down in an empty time slot for that afternoon.

You had to take Music 1 unless you were in band, orchestra, or chorus. Three days in the class had been enough. Yvonne couldn't play an instrument, but she knew she could sing. She was already starting to think about her presentation for the chorus director.

"All right, *that* was better," Mr. Yesler said. It was six weeks later. "You're finally sounding like a chorus, and just in time, with the Thanksgiving concert coming up. Now let's try it up to tempo. That means full speed ahead," he added. There were laughs.

"Sopranos, you're doing a good job getting up to those high notes, but make sure you stay there. Don't go sliding down. Nice blend, first altos. Flawless."

Mr. Yesler raised his baton. "All right, ready?"

Yvonne breathed in silently, one of the chorus.

Harcourt

Mr. Yesler had Yvonne sing some scales. Then he set a piece of music on the piano and asked her to read it. It was a folk tune, "Red River Valley," exactly the kind of thing she hated about Music 1. Folk music, opera—who cared? But she knew the song from fifth grade, and she sang it in a lilting up-to-date style.

Finally Mr. Yesler had her sing a song of her own choosing. Now she could cut loose. Her powerful yet melodious voice boomed off the walls of the room.

2

"Last year the Authentics came out to help boost ticket sales for the talent show," Sara said. "They did two of their old hits—a bunch of grandpas." She laughed. "They'd started singing together in a school chorus forty years ago. That's why Mr. Yesler does this. He says music is a legacy from one generation to the next."

Yvonne was still silent. It was the first time she'd considered that adults must have had dreams once, just like hers. Some, like Mr. Yesler, had persevered, and now they were realizing new dreams.

"Okay, Sara," Yvonne said slowly, "tell me what a perfect fifth is."

11

Harcourt

In spite of herself, Yvonne joined in:

—*From all this rock and roll . . .*

The girls laughed. "There, you see?" said Sara.

"You're pretty good," Yvonne said grudgingly. "You have a very melodious voice—very lilting."

"You're pretty good too," said Sara. "But what do we do in a few years when that sound is a dinosaur too?"

Yvonne just looked at her.

"Look, Mr. Yesler doesn't teach us *his* kind of singing," Sara said. "He teaches us *singing*. I mean, I didn't get it right away either, but when you can do what he's trying to teach us, you can sing anything."

"Very nice," Mr. Yesler said. "I'll put you down for first alto. Can you read music?"

"Sure," Yvonne said.

"Great. A lot of kids come in here not knowing how, so it may be a little slow for you at first. One more thing, Yvonne. You gave a fine presentation just now, but remember, this is choral singing. It's not a place for headliners. Do you understand what I'm saying?"

"Sure."

"Then I'll see you at two-fifteen Monday." Mr. Yesler smiled and shook her hand.

Harcourt

"Yesler?" Yvonne's father asked that evening. "That isn't Clarence Yesler, is it?"

"I don't know his first name," Yvonne said.

"I heard he was a teacher now," Papa said. "That's quite a musical legacy you've got at your school."

"Who's Clarence Yesler?"

Her father leafed through a stack of albums, old-fashioned recordings of thirty years ago. He picked one up. "Is this your Mr. Yesler?" he asked.

"Wow!" Yvonne said.

4

"*His* kind of singing?" Sara smiled. "What do you know about Mr. Yesler?"

"Clarence and the Authentics. Not bad, if you like dance music from the age of dinosaurs."

"Okay, so you know. Look, he had the kind of musical career you dream about, and now—"

"How do you know what my dreams are?"

"Because they're my dreams too. Hit records. Big crowds." Sara threw her head back and sang:

Can't stop this feeling!

My heart is reeling—

9

Three days later Yvonne and Sara were alone in the music room. "Okay, so I lied," Yvonne said. "I can't read music. I don't know what any of that stuff means—major third, perfect whatever. I just know I made a perfect idiot of myself."

"Don't worry about it," Sara said. "Most of us come into this chorus not knowing any of that. Mr. Yesler's a good teacher."

"Not for me," Yvonne said bitterly. "I can sing. I just don't care about *his* kind of singing."

"Deep breath in . . . slow hiss out," Mr. Yesler said. "Remember, singing starts with breathing. That's fine. Flawless! Now, very lightly, on 'Ooo. . . .'"

This was not what Yvonne had expected chorus to be like. They spent the first fifteen minutes of each rehearsal doing warm-ups. That wasn't singing, any more than jumping jacks were volleyball.

"Okay, let's do the Bach chorale. Watch your dynamics. Remember, those two *p*'s mean 'very soft.'"

And the music was just the sort of stuff she hated— Bach, Mozart, cowboy songs! Still, she had persevered for two weeks so far.

Mr. Yesler called Yvonne over to the piano as the class ended. Sara Katel was standing with him.

"Yes?" said Yvonne.

"I wonder if you'd be willing to work with Sara one-on-one for a while," the chorus director said. "You're a fine singer, but I think you need a little help with ear training and sight singing."

Yvonne's cheeks burned. She didn't want, didn't need, any help from Ms. Perfect. Sara was an eighth grader, one of the school's "stars."

"I don't think I need help," Yvonne said.

"No?" Mr. Yesler played a note on the piano. "Sing a perfect fifth above that," he said.

Yvonne sang a note.

Mr. Yesler played another note. "Sing a major third below that."

Yvonne sang. She saw Sara look away, embarrassed.

Mr. Yesler put a sheet of music on the piano. "Could you sing me the first alto line, please?"

Yvonne turned and ran from the room.

Harcourt

Fingertips

by David Gallash
illustrated by Lee Anne Levin

Fold

TAKE-HOME BOOK
Times of Discovery
Use with "Out of Darkness: The Story of Louis Braille"

Harcourt

Harcourt

Meeting the Challenge

Louis had to think of a creative way to finish his newspaper assignment. Think of a time when you were faced with a new challenge and had to find a solution. On a separate sheet of paper, write a paragraph describing the experience.

School-Home Connection Listen as your child reads this book aloud. Then talk with your child about how Louis proved himself. Compare thoughts about ways that you both have had to prove yourselves.

Harcourt

"The *Messenger*'s here!" students called across the snow-covered lawn.

It was December 1. Most of the staff had returned a day or two late, but the paper was out on time.

"You changed my copy!" Mark said to Louis, but he was smiling.

"Well, you said it was rough," Louis said, but he was smiling too.

"I think Stein has earned himself a place on the first team," Mark said. The other staff members agreed. "We usually don't give seventh graders jobs like this, but here's what I'd like you to do for the next issue. . . ."

Soccer practice had gone on longer than usual, and Louis was late for the meeting. All the eighth graders on the staff were already there—Cheryl, Seth, Shelby, and Mark. Especially Mark.

"So," Mark was saying, "you all have your assignments. Now we're running that big ad for Bramson's Sport Shop, so we need to have the issue out by December 1. If there's anyone who can't get copy to me by the Monday after Thanksgiving, you'd better let me know now."

Louis tried to slip into the room, but Mark turned at the sound of his footsteps. "Oh, here you are, Stein," he said. "Glad you showed up. I need to talk to you about that interview with Coach Fuller."

Louis's cheeks burned. *Glad you showed up.* As if he ever missed a meeting! Usually he came early, hoping Mark would give him a choice assignment.

He watched Mark tap his stylus on the Braille board. How could he do it with any precision when he never seemed to stop talking? But when Mark transcribed his copy into the computer, it always came out right.

The power was still out that evening, so Louis had to work by candlelight.

He checked every word for the sake of precision. Gradually he became familiar with the patterns of dots. It was slow going, but he began to feel as though he were reading with his fingertips. He tried it with his eyes closed but gave up quickly.

It's a lot harder than it looks, he thought.

Harcourt

Harcourt

Louis found a chart showing the Braille alphabet. In the fourth grade he had been fascinated with secret codes. That made the job a little easier.

If Brovar had left a copy on a floppy disk, Louis thought, I wouldn't have to be doing this. I could have edited this on the laptop and printed it later. I've got to talk to him about that.

"Sorry," Mark told him later. "I already gave out everything. Maybe next issue." He spread the printed sheets on the table. "I had to change your basketball piece," he said. He ran his fingertips over his copy of what Louis had written. "Here we are. When did you talk to Coach Fuller?"

"I don't know. Last Tuesday, I guess," Louis said.

"Before the injury to Bruce Dowling?"

"I guess so. He didn't say anything about Dowling being injured."

"When there are new developments on a story, you should always follow them up," Mark said. "Everything the coach said about this new offense he's devised around Dowling will have to be changed now."

Later that afternoon Louis discussed the school paper situation with his mother. "I don't need this," Louis told her. "I'm going to quit the paper. It's hard enough keeping up with schoolwork and soccer. I don't need to get put down by Mark Brovar. All the good story assignments go to the boarding students, who live in the dormitory—Mark's friends."

"Aren't they all older kids, too?" his mother asked.

"Well, yes, but why can't he give a seventh grader a chance? He never lets me show what I can do!"

The buses weren't running. Louis pushed his way through the drifted snow to the George Academy.

In Mark's dormitory room Louis found the pile of paper with the raised dots. Beside it was Mark's stylus. He saw that Mark's computer had Braille dots on all the keys. There was a Braille printer on the shelf next to the standard printer.

Someone's obviously devised a program to print regular files in Braille, Louis thought. He'd have to ask Mark to show him how it worked.

Harcourt

Harcourt

"Uh, Mark?" said Louis.

"What?"

"You have a hard copy anywhere? The power is out. I can't open your file or run your printer."

There was silence on the phone.

"Brovar? You still there?"

"Yes," Mark said slowly. "Yes, there's a hard copy on my desk, but it's not transcribed. It's in Braille."

Louis gave the matter a few moments' thought.

"Well, I can try," he said.

8

"Louis, you knew things would be tougher at George Academy," his mother said. "You worked hard to get that scholarship. If being a star is so important to you, there are plenty of other schools around."

"That's not fair, Mom," Louis said.

"How long have you been at George?"

"You know how long."

"Three months, and that's not very long. You're making good grades, and you're making friends. You'll prove yourself there. I know you will. Just accept that it's going to happen gradually."

Louis hoped his mother was right. Sometimes he felt as if he would never fit in at his new school.

5

Thanksgiving Day was cloudy and cold. On Friday snow began to fall. By Saturday the wind had whipped it into a blizzard. The weather people called it the worst November storm in the city's history.

By Sunday morning 20 inches had fallen and electric power was out across a wide area.

The phone call came just after noon.

"Stein, am I glad I caught you!" said a familiar voice.

"Brovar?" said Louis.

"Right," said Mark. "Listen, I need a tremendous favor. Could you print out and edit some very rough copy from my computer at the dormitory?"

"Sure," Louis began, "but—"

"That's great!" said Mark. "The file name is 'messenger twelve-dot-one.' I'm glad I could find a day student to do this. The airport is closed because of the storm, and I'm stuck here at home. I don't know when anyone's going to be getting back to school, and I need—"

6

7

Harcourt

TAKE-HOME BOOK
Times of Discovery
Use with "Anne of Green Gables."

Visiting Anne's House

by Elaine Roche-Tombee
illustrated by Mary Bollinger

Fold

Design a Tourist Attraction

Choose a character from a favorite book. On a separate sheet of paper, design a home for your character. Write or draw an ad inviting people to tour the home.

Fold

School-Home Connection Listen as your child reads this book aloud. Then talk with your child about which characters in books have seemed almost real to both of you. What makes a fictional character seem real?

Her name was Anne Shirley. She had bright-red hair and a terrible temper. She was quick to become exasperated if you spelled her name without the *e*. People often wore bewildered expressions when she used big words. Still, people have found her irresistible for nearly a hundred years.

Anne grew up in Avonlea, on Canada's Prince Edward Island. Visitors today tour Green Gables, the house she lived in. They walk the paths of this small community that has changed little since Anne's day.

A Japanese travel magazine once asked its readers where they would most like to visit. The leading vote-getters were New York, Paris, and London. In fourth place was Prince Edward Island.

All of the attention she receives might send even Anne into a fluster. Then again, perhaps she would be delighted to know she has so many fans.

Of course, she would probably call them "kindred spirits."

Harcourt

There's one thing wrong with this picture—well, actually, several things. Anne Shirley never lived in Avonlea. In fact, there is no Avonlea, and Anne never lived at all. She is a fictional character. She first appeared in *Anne of Green Gables*, a book by Lucy Maud Montgomery.

Even so, tourists flock to the town "where Anne grew up." They peep into Anne's room. They dress up in Anne's clothes. They laugh at the cracked writing slate that Anne broke over the head of a boy who teased her. They solemnly exchange wedding vows by the fireplace where Anne's creator herself was married.

Visitors from Japan are among Anne's greatest fans. *Anne of Green Gables* was translated into Japanese in 1954. Japanese children read it as part of their middle-school program. Many young women in Japan read the book again when applying for jobs. They hope to be inspired by Anne's honesty and courage.

A full-sized model of the Green Gables house stands in a Japanese theme park. There are Anne cartoons on Japanese TV. There is even a school for learning English called the Anne Academy.

Harcourt

Anne's fans find the experience sublime. People who have never read *Anne of Green Gables* are often bewildered. How did the home of a made-up person become a tourist attraction?

Prince Edward Island is Canada's smallest province. There is no Avonlea, but there is a town called Cavendish on the island's north shore.

Anne's story is dramatically portrayed in *Anne of Green Gables: The Musical*. The play has run on Prince Edward Island every summer since 1965.

In another show, *Anne and Diana*, audiences laugh as Anne's best friend becomes exasperated with Anne's temper. They smile as Anne begs for forgiveness. The play is part of a Lucy Maud Montgomery Festival held every August.

Harcourt

Lucy Maud Montgomery was born on Prince Edward Island in 1874. She was raised by grandparents in Cavendish. She attended college and later taught school and worked for a newspaper. She also wrote poems and stories. In 1908 she published *Anne of Green Gables*, her first novel.

In the book, the aging bachelor Matthew Cuthbert and his sister, Marilla, send for an orphan child to help out on their farm. They are expecting a boy. Instead, they get a girl— eleven-year-old Anne.

The "Anne tour" includes a ride in "Matthew's buggy." A horse draws the carriage around the pond that Anne's imagination turned into the sublime "Lake of Shining Waters."

At the Anne of Green Gables store, tourists buy Anne dolls. They tour the factory where the dolls are made. They buy *Anne* books and Anne hats, even Anne snacks. They explore the forest Anne spoke of. They walk down the cow path she walked down.

Harcourt

At first Anne tends to put the Cuthberts into a fluster, and Marilla wants to send her back. But Anne soon wins them over. Her imagination and her sunny personality dramatically brighten the lives of the people of Avonlea.

Anne of Green Gables was an immediate success in Canada and the United States. Children's books of the early 1900s tended to preach solemnly at their readers. When these books are read today, their characters seem false.

In all, Lucy Maud Montgomery wrote more than twenty books. She died in 1942. Five years earlier, Canada had made Green Gables a national park. The town of Cavendish, population 196, now hosts hundreds of thousands of visitors each year.

The house and grounds have been lovingly restored in great detail. Furniture of the early 1900s shares space with items suggested by the *Anne* books, such as the cracked slate.

Harcourt

Anne, in contrast, was fun and playful. Her approach to life was irresistible. She faced the world with courage and honesty. Like real children, Anne sought to "invent herself" outside the strict world in which she was brought up. Adults liked the character too, for her sense of responsibility toward others.

In writing *Anne*, Montgomery drew on her own experiences. Cavendish became Avonlea, and its people became Anne's neighbors. The Cuthberts' house, Green Gables, was modeled on the home of Montgomery's cousins.

Anne of Green Gables continues to sell. It has never been out of print. It has sold more than nine million copies and has been translated into seventeen languages. *Anne of Avonlea*, the first of six sequels, appeared in 1909.

The first movie based on *Anne of Green Gables* came out in 1919. Several others followed. No fewer than three TV serials based on the *Anne* books have been produced. The 1985 version was Canada's most-watched TV series ever.

Harcourt

6

7

Harcourt

TAKE-HOME BOOK
Times of Discovery
Use with "Cowboys: Roundup on an American Ranch."

Answers:
1. F 2. T 3. F 4. T 5. T 6. T 7. F 8. F 9. F 10. T

Bronco Buster

by Dusty Chapman
illustrated by K. Bowser

True or False

What did you learn about Billy Harder's life from this book? Number a sheet of paper from 1 to 10. Then for each statement below, write *T* or *F* next to its number to show whether it is true or false. (Answers are on the back of this page.)

___ 1. Billy was thirteen when he left home.

___ 2. At first, Billy didn't think of himself as a cowboy.

___ 3. Ty was six years older than Billy.

___ 4. Ty didn't think the cowboy life would last.

___ 5. Billy was in Kansas when he wrote to his dad and mom.

___ 6. A girl got Billy's horse.

___ 7. The winter of 1886–1887 was one of the best for Texas cattle ranchers.

___ 8. Billy and the other cowboys captured no more than thirty horses.

___ 9. Billy never did well at breaking horses.

___ 10. Buffalo Bill Cody and Sitting Bull were very famous men.

School-Home Connection Listen as your child reads this book aloud. Then discuss the characters with your child. Did they seem true to life? Why or why not?

Fold

Harcourt

Since then Ty and I have been all over the country. I even had my dad and mom take a train to Omaha, Nebraska, to see one of our shows.

They were both thrilled. My dad was especially thrilled at shaking the hands of Buffalo Bill Cody and Sitting Bull.

Before Dad and Mom left on their train trip home, I took them out to dinner at a fine restaurant. Dad said that he always knew I was going to make something of myself. Mom said that I was beginning to look a lot like Dad.

As for me, I was just glad to see their craggy faces once more.

12

My dad had a craggy face. I first noticed it on the day he turned me out. It was March 24, 1886—my fourteenth birthday.

"You're grown up, Billy Harder," he said. "Your mom and I figure it's time for you to move on. You've learned all you can on our little ranch."

I was glad to hear his words. For a time, I'd been feeling as corralled as the horses. I was anxious to ride west and make a life of my own.

The next morning I kissed my mom good-bye and took off. Her tear-stained face was a little craggy, too. Ranch life was rough on her and Dad.

1

Within a week I had my first full-fledged job. It was riding herd on some longhorns being moved north to the railroad at Wichita, Kansas.

I did some of the things that a cowboy does. There were always a few cows that wandered off, but we couldn't allow any diversion from the trail. I had to round up those strays along with an ornery cow or two. The strays were easy enough to handle, but I sometimes needed help with an ornery cow.

That was how Ty Webber and I became friends. He was twenty-two and had been a full-fledged cowboy for six years. Ornery cows were no match for Ty. No matter how wild they were, they soon became compliant for him.

2

Then one day Buffalo Bill Cody appeared at the corral in person. He'd come to see me break a horse, and I became mighty nervous about that.

Nervous or not, I did my riding and took my thumps. Later, the rancher told me that Mr. Cody wanted to see me.

He told me about a new thing they were having in his Wild West Show. It was called bronco busting, and he wanted me to have a starring role.

I couldn't refuse. I took the job and even managed to talk him into hiring Ty as a cowboy in the show.

11

Harcourt

Of course, I'd broken my own horse, but that was it.
I really didn't know if I was meant for the job, but I soon
found out.

I loved it! When I told that to the other cowboys,
they acted as if I were crazy. It was just a job to them,
and a tough one at that.

To me, it was fun. I even enjoyed the hard knocks. I
felt as if I'd been born to break horses.

The horses seemed to sense the way I felt. They
gave me a fair share of hard tosses, but they also
quickly became compliant. I didn't realize it at the time,
but I was building a reputation for this kind of work.

Ty had been turned out when he was thirteen, and
he always missed his little brother. I suppose that's why
he took a liking to me.

After a while Ty taught me how to deal with the
ornery cows instead of doing the job himself. He taught
me other things, too—things he'd learned on cattle
drives all over Texas.

With lessons from Ty, I figured I might be able to
pass for a cowboy by the time we reached Wichita.
Unfortunately, Ty's lessons came with a warning. He said
that cowboys were a dying breed. Farms with fences
spelled the end for
cattle drives.

Harcourt

Wichita, Kansas, was the biggest town I'd ever seen, and I stayed there for about a month. By that time my money was running low, but luck was with me. I managed to sign on for another cattle drive in the spring. This time I was going to get cowboy wages. I was proud of myself. So I sent off a letter to Dad and Mom before riding back to Texas.

On the way I decided to trade my horse. I loved her, but Ty had warned me that she wasn't right for cowboy work. I didn't want to overwork her, but I wasn't about to trade her until I was sure she'd have a good home.

We ran into a herd of forty or so mustangs on the open range near the big ranch. As luck had it, they were a gentle bunch, and we managed to drive them into a large corral on the ranch.

The ranch owner was delighted and paid right up.

With money in our pockets and a good home-cooked meal in our bellies, we got ready to set out after more strays.

The rancher had another idea. He wanted to hire us on to break horses. Ty and the others turned him down. They didn't like getting tossed off horses. I thought I could stand it, so I stayed on at the ranch.

Harcourt

Our money was about to run out when Ty got wind of some work. A big rancher over in the Texas panhandle was buying up wild mustangs and paying a good price per head.

According to what we learned, the rancher was buying up the stray horses for Buffalo Bill Cody's Wild West Show.

So Ty and I headed for the panhandle. Along the way we picked up a couple of other cowboys to ride with us. They, too, were out of work because of the disastrous winter.

One day, just after I reached the Texas border, I stayed at a small ranch. At breakfast I mentioned wanting to trade my horse.

The rancher was interested. He wanted a compliant, older horse for his young daughter. He offered to let me take my pick of the wild horses he had corralled there. Of course, I'd have to break the horse I picked.

I'd helped my dad break horses, but I'd never really broken one myself. Still, I didn't see it as the hardest job in the world. I picked a big brown colt, and the rancher put it into a smaller corral.

Harcourt

The diversion from the big corral didn't sit well with the colt. He was pretty fired up when I got close to him, and roping him was a real job. After a while he calmed down a little, but the day I could actually ride him seemed a long way off.

The rancher didn't mind. He had space for me, and I did a few chores to pay for my meals. In the meantime, watching me try to break the colt promised to amuse him and the ranch hands.

To their surprise it took me only a little over a week to throw my saddle onto the colt. Two days later I was riding him. When we left, I waved good-bye to the rancher's daughter. She was on my old horse.

Ty and I hooked up again in Texas. We'd both signed on for the same cattle drive and were waiting for the long, hard winter to end.

When it did end, we got some bad news. Most of the cattle were dead. Their bodies were lying on the range. It was a sorry sight.

I never did forget the sight of all those dead cattle in the spring thaw. It permeates all my memories of that time, the way that smoke permeates a closed room.

For Ty and me, that disastrous winter of 1886–1887 meant we weren't going on a cattle drive anytime soon.

Harcourt

TAKE-HOME BOOK
Times of Discovery
Use with "The Wright Brothers."

Fold

The Sky Above, the Earth Below

by Isabel Gallego
illustrated by B. Walker

You're a Poet

On a separate sheet of paper, write a short poem about something you love to do.

Fold

School-Home Connection Listen as your child reads this poem aloud. Then talk with your child about how the author describes the experience of piloting a small plane. How do her words make the reader understand what she feels?

Oh, give me wings, an engine, rudder true,
My hand at the controls to guide me through,
And once again among the clouds I'll go,
Between the sky above and earth below!

Oh, give me wings, enabling me to soar
Where few but birds have ever gone before.
Just my machine and I, aloft we go,
Between the sky above and earth below!

Your engine gleams, all solid, strong, and clean,
Your tank is filled with high-test gasoline.
Your stick and rudder steady in my hands,
Your instruments awaiting my commands.

Contact! Your engine roars, I feel its power,
I get the "okay" signal from the tower.
We gather speed; then, hoisted by the breeze,
We're airborne—rising fast—we've cleared the trees!

Too soon, we must return—don't be too slow.
Your endurance is mighty, but your fuel runs low.
Turn, brave machine! Turn now, and carve the air!
Too soon must end this airborne joy we share.

Follow the river, from the mountain's dome;
It guides me to a swift and sure way home.
Follow it over forest, field, and town,
Enabling me to find my safe way down.

Harcourt

Nose up! Earth falls away before my eyes.
Bank left! We hang suspended in the skies.
I dance with the horizon, first left, then right.
Then I level off and set my course for flight.

"Come follow me!" the river seems to call,
"Beyond the city, mill, and waterfall.
Follow me, wherever that you will.
Your ship has the endurance, you the skill."

— Fold —

Harcourt

Can there be a more grand and glorious place,
This ceiling of the earth, this floor of space?
Could there be so magnificent a sight
As that which greets my eyes on this high flight?

Below, the busy city seems a toy,
Assembled by a clever girl or boy:
Toy cars, toy buildings, a delight to see,
In perfect scale and fine geometry.

Toy people too—they stop when I pass by,
Leave off their work and look up at the sky
In wonder and in envy, feeling bound,
Inseparable from earth and solid ground.

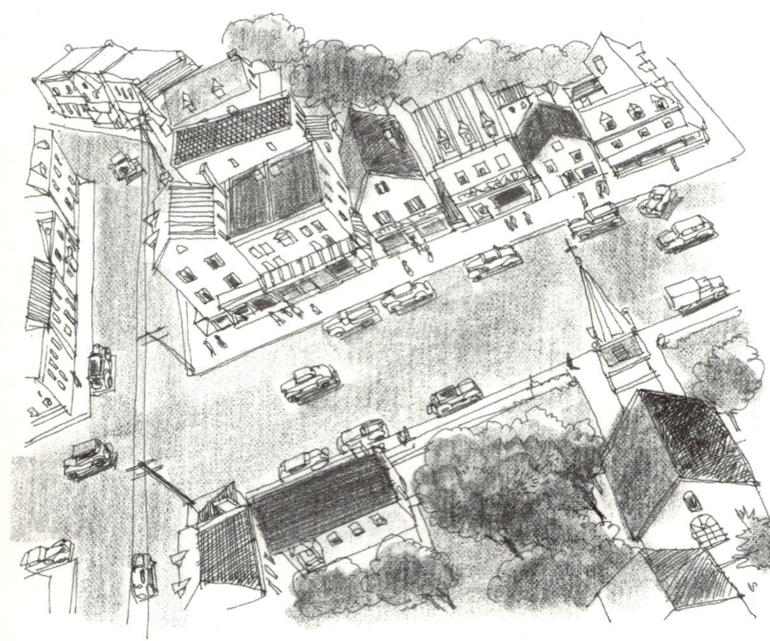

Buffeted by the wind, higher I fly,
To seek a gentler layer of the sky.
Weather and wind remind me, here alone,
This world above the earth is not my own.

Yet there are dangers up, and dangers down:
Defeat, a cruel word, a scornful frown.
When buffeted by cares, I find release
In the sky's splendor and the clouds' peace.

Harcourt

Our shadow, passing swiftly on the land,
Reveals us to be partners, hand in hand.
Inseparable are my machine and I,
As river from its banks, or sun from sky.

Or do they dream, as once I dreamed of flight,
Watching the birds and wishing that I might
Be hoisted up to join them? Now it's true,
For what we can imagine, we can do!

One thousand feet below, the earth seems still.
All's peaceful in each field and on each hill.
The works of nature are in perfect order,
Human works too, within each fence and border.

This is a sight that few have ever seen,
The world in pattern, brown and blue and green.
It's spread out all before me, all as one—
A whole new way of seeing has begun.

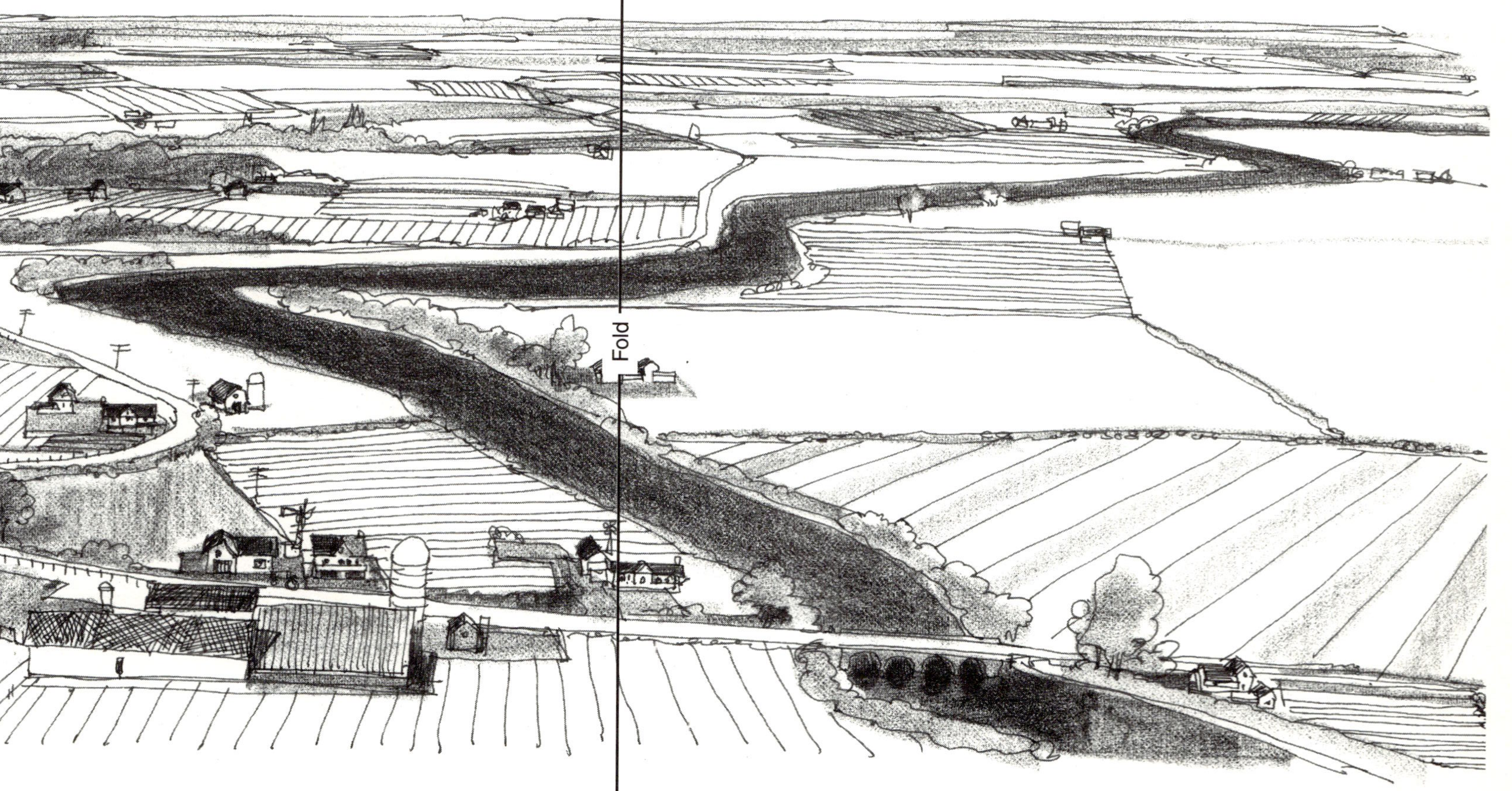

Harcourt

Harcourt

TAKE-HOME BOOK
Times of Discovery
Use with "I Want to Be an Astronaut."

The Three Orbits of John Glenn

by Karen Stamfil
illustrated by John Anthony Dollar

Harcourt

Ask an Astronaut

Suppose you could ask John Glenn one question about his spaceflight experience. What would your question be? Write it on a sheet of paper.

Fold

School-Home Connection Listen as your child reads this book aloud. Many people have called John Glenn a hero. What are your child's thoughts and your own about what makes a person heroic?

In October 1998, at the age of seventy-seven, John Glenn became the oldest person ever to leave planet Earth. The senator from Ohio was part of the crew of the space shuttle *Discovery*. His mission was to test how well a person his age could perform in space flight.

Glenn performed splendidly, but that was no surprise. Space travel was nothing new to him. And *Discovery*'s high-tech facilities were far more comfortable than those he'd had on his previous trip.

Four hours, fifty-five minutes. *Friendship 7* splashes down in the Atlantic. The recovery ship has sighted it. Minutes later the ship is alongside.

Glenn feels the capsule rubbing against the side of the ship. He feels it lifted into the air. There is a bump. Glenn warns the crew to stand clear. He blows the door off the capsule with explosive bolts.

Sailors reach in to help him out. John Glenn stands on the deck of the ship, back on planet Earth.

Harcourt

Harcourt

Cape Canaveral, Florida, February 20, 1962. John Glenn is about to become the first American to orbit the Earth. It is 9:47 A.M. Glenn's fellow astronaut Alan Shepard counts down: "Three, two, one, *zero!*"

The engines fire. The rocket lifts off the ground. Through the window of his *Friendship 7* space capsule, Glenn sees the horizon turning.

The rocket accelerates. It bursts out of the atmosphere. Glenn is pressed back into his seat. He now weighs nearly 1,000 pounds. He has experienced this feeling many times during flight simulation.

Flaming pieces of metal rush past the window. Is it the burned-out retrorockets? Or is it the heat shield? Is the capsule itself beginning to burn up?

"This is *Friendship 7*. A real fireball outside." But Glenn sounds cool as communication is restored, and he talks with Cape Canaveral. He drops below 100,000 feet, back into the atmosphere.

Four hours, forty-nine minutes. Ten thousand feet. The main parachute opens. It is hot inside the capsule, but now vents open and fresh air comes in from outside.

Friendship 7 slows down to a safe landing speed.

Harcourt

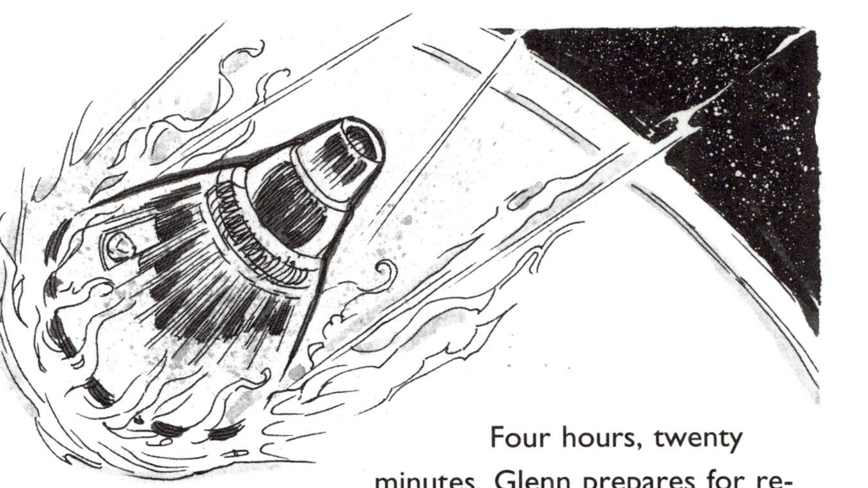

Four hours, twenty
minutes. Glenn prepares for re-
entry. After more tests, it is decided that the landing bag
signal must have been false. But no one is sure.

Four hours, thirty-three minutes. Glenn fires *Friendship 7*'s
retrorockets[3]. They slow the capsule down and break it out of
orbit. Glenn keeps it in position by hand control. He brings it
level with the Earth.

Four hours, forty-three minutes. Communication with
Earth is broken briefly while *Friendship 7* enters the
atmosphere. Through the window Glenn sees a brilliant
orange glow. No simulation could have prepared him for this.
Friction is heating the capsule to 3,000°F.

---

[3]**retro** reverse

Nearly five minutes
into the flight, the capsule
separates from the rocket. For
a moment Glenn feels as if he's been shot forward. Then he
feels himself lifted out of his seat. "Zero g,[1] and I feel fine,"
he reports.

Friendship 7 turns 180 degrees. Glenn is now facing
backward as he orbits the Earth. He tests the system for
controlling the ship's position. He can either let it be set
automatically or maneuver *Friendship 7* himself. This will be
vital at the end of the flight. The capsule must be in the
correct position when it reenters the atmosphere, or Glenn
will not get home.

---

[1]**zero g** "zero gravity": weightlessness

Glenn's speed in orbit is nearly five miles a second.
Eighteen minutes into the flight, *Friendship 7* approaches the
coast of Africa.

Glenn runs medical tests and experiments. He reports to
a tracking station in the Canary Islands. These stations are
placed around the Earth so that Glenn will never be out of
contact while in orbit.

Forty minutes into the flight, Glenn sees the sun set over
the Indian Ocean. It seems to melt into a bright white band
and spread out over the horizon. The strip of light grows
darker and smaller. Then it fades
out completely.

More than three hours into the flight now. Glenn passes
over the United States for the second time and begins his
third and last orbit.

"I can see the whole state of Florida, just laid out like a
map," he reports. "It's beautiful." He takes photographs with
several types of cameras. He passes again into night and then
back into daylight for the last time.

The automatic control system has not worked well since
the beginning of the flight. Glenn can maneuver the capsule
back into the correct position, but it keeps swinging back to
the right.

Harcourt

Harcourt

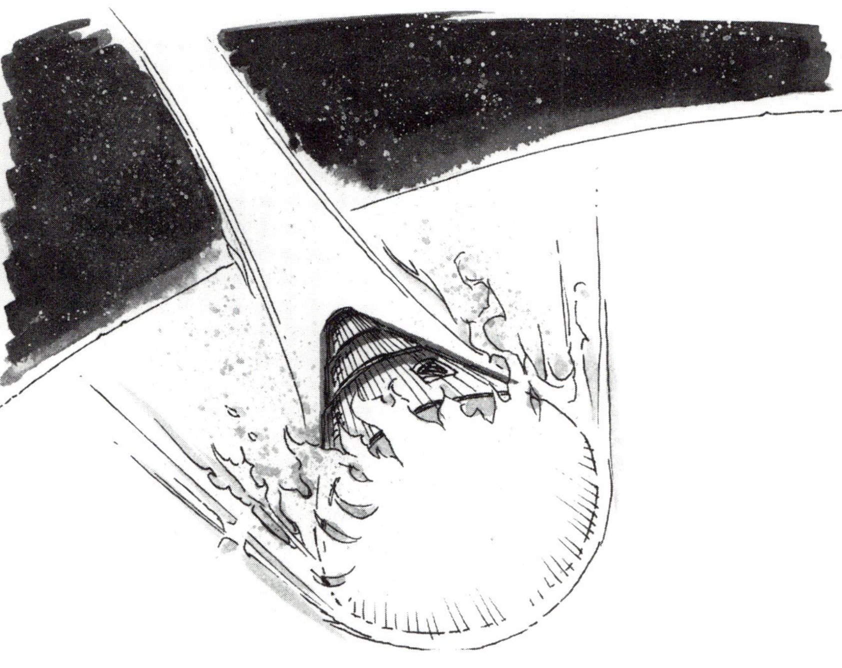

In space, Glenn finishes his first orbit. He passes back over the Atlantic toward Africa again.

Halfway through his second orbit, Glenn is told of the possible problem with the landing bag. He has had no sign that the bag is down, but he grasps the problem at once. If the heat shield is loose, it cannot protect him from the blazing heat of reentry into the atmosphere.

Glenn is now on the night side of Earth. He takes out a star navigation device. This is not high-tech equipment. It is a simple star chart with a plastic slide over it. He lines up the slide with a time scale. This shows him the stars he should be seeing.

There they are. That's the constellation Aries at the top of the window. Astronauts will be able to find their position by star navigation, just as oceangoing sailors do.

At NASA's[2] mission control facilities, Glenn's orbit is tracked on a map. As he passes over Perth, Australia, the people of the city turn on their lights as a signal to him. They will do so again thirty-six years later.

Glenn runs more tests. He eats from a squeeze tube. Behind him, the sun comes up. He is over the Pacific Ocean, an hour and a quarter into the flight. He passes over Mexico, nearing the end of his first orbit.

Meanwhile, NASA engineers are worried. A radio signal seems to show that *Friendship 7*'s landing bag has dropped into position. This is not supposed to happen until just before landing. The bag acts as a cushion when the capsule lands in the ocean. If the signal is correct, it means that the heat shield is loose, too.

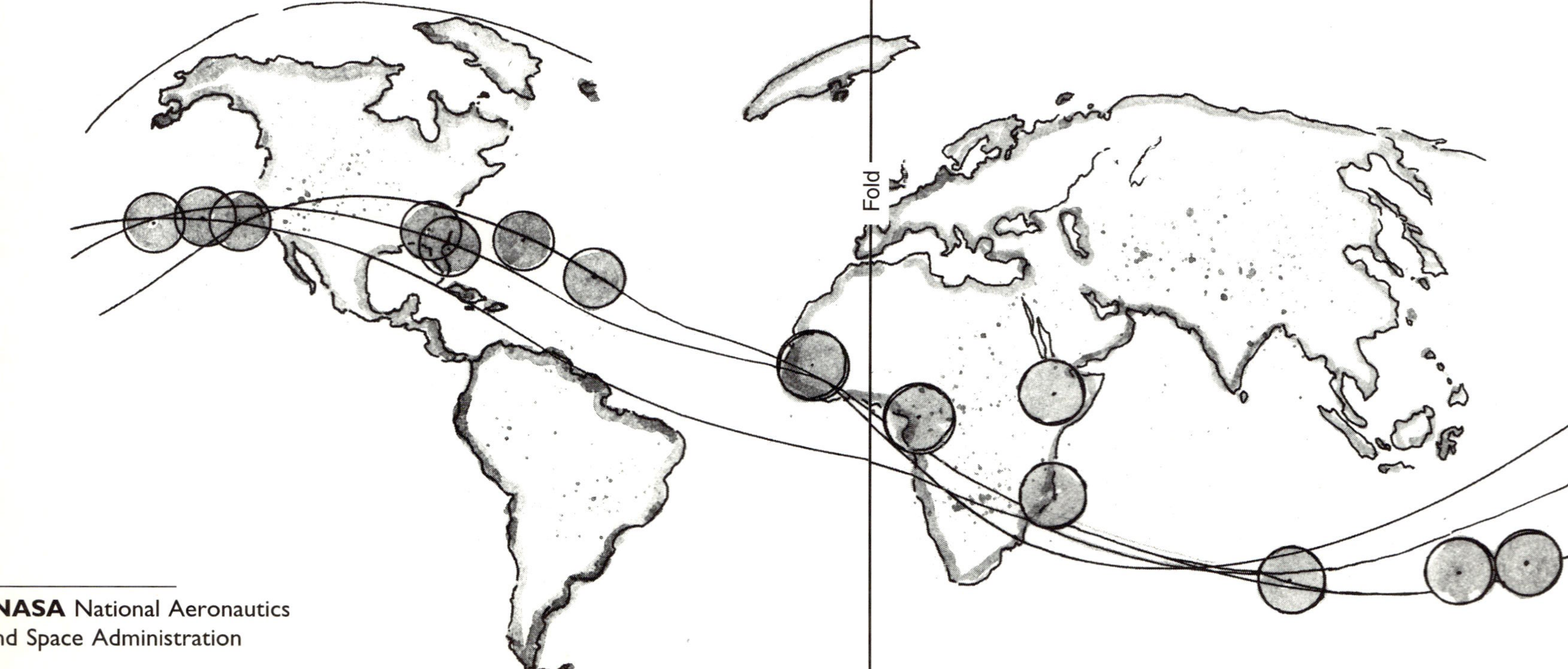

[2]**NASA** National Aeronautics
and Space Administration

Harcourt

Harcourt

TAKE-HOME BOOK
Times of Discovery
Use with "Voyager."

— Fold —

Science Unfair!

by Joseph Lehmann
illustrated by Anne Borowski

Discover Something New

Learning new things is fun and rewarding. Think about a science project you had to do and the new things you learned from it. On a separate sheet of paper, make a list of new facts you learned by doing the science project.

School-Home Connection Listen as your child reads this book aloud. Then with your child, brainstorm ways he or she could find help in doing a science project.

Harcourt

"This is Dr. Alison Baird," Caroline said. The red-haired woman stepped forward and smiled. "She's a scientist who's been studying Io since the *Voyager* missions. In fact, even before *Voyager*, she predicted that Io would have volcanoes. Thank you, Dr. Baird."

"You're welcome, Caroline," the scientist said. She looked at the class. "In case you're wondering," she said, "Noah e-mailed me and asked for my help. You see, I've known his mom forever. We went to school together."

There was a moment of silence. "That's *unfair*!" Tim said. Then everyone laughed.

"So what's wrong with Io?" Linda demanded.

"Nothing's *wrong* with it," Noah said. "It's pretty cool, actually, with all those volcanoes. I'm just not sure how much recent information about Io we'll be able to find."

"Noah's right," said Caroline. "Mr. Saenz wants to see stuff that's been discovered about our moon since the *Voyager* missions. What's new about Io?"

Harcourt

Caroline, Linda, and Noah were sitting at the kitchen table in Caroline's apartment, planning their project for the sixth-grade science fair.

"Well, there's the *Galileo* mission," Linda said. She fanned out a pile of brightly colored papers on the table. "I got these telescopic pictures from the Internet. *Galileo*'s transmitters must be more powerful than *Voyager*'s. Look at these!"

"They're newer," said Caroline. "Those pictures were taken in 1997."

"But they show the same old volcanoes," said Noah.

When the group finished its presentation, there was applause from the class.

"Does anyone have any questions for Group Io?" Mr. Saenz asked. Hands went up. "Tim?"

"I'd like to know where they got that video," Tim said. There was agreement from the class.

"We made it," Linda said.

There were expressions of disbelief.

"It's true," said Noah. "Of course, we had a *little* help."

Harcourt

"Now *why* does Io have all those volcanoes?" asked Noah. The video showed another simulation.

"The answer probably has to do with gravity," Noah explained. "We all know how the moon's gravity causes ocean tides on Earth. Well, Jupiter's gravity causes *huge* tides, only there's no water, and Ganymede and Europa are pulling the other way. This creates lots of heat and all that energy has to go somewhere."

"Not exactly," said Linda. "This report says that *Galileo* discovered hundreds of volcanic openings. And look at this lava flow. It formed in the time it took *Galileo* to make just a few orbits around Jupiter, and it's as big as Arizona. And the lava is 3,000 degrees Fahrenheit—hotter than any volcano on Earth."

"Okay," said Caroline, "those are some good facts and numbers that we can use. Now what I'd like to find is something—I don't know, like a picture of one of Io's volcanoes erupting."

"Or being shattered by a collision with an asteroid," Noah offered.

Harcourt

"Where could we get something like that?" sighed Linda.

"I don't know—call a scientist?" said Caroline. "This Alison Baird who wrote the Internet report—maybe she's got stuff she could send us."

"Alison Baird!" Noah grabbed the page from Caroline and stared at the name on the top. A grin broke out on his face. "I think we just might be able to find what we're looking for!" he said.

"Io has an iron core, just like Earth," Linda said. "But volcanoes and iron are about all that are similar between Io and Earth. Take their atmospheres, for example. Io's is mostly sulfur dioxide—a deadly poison spewed out by the volcanoes. Actually, the atmospheres of all of Jupiter's moons are pretty deadly."

"Most of the lava is melted silica—like sand or glass," Caroline continued. "There are a lot of metals in it too. Scientists think Earth had volcanoes like this back in the early days, and maybe Mars and Venus did too."

Harcourt

Here the video turned into a jerky series of pictures. This was no simulation but actual telescopic photographs. Io looked like a holiday ornament that had been shattered by a collision with a sidewalk and glued back together.

"These pictures were sent to Earth by *Galileo*'s transmitters," Noah said.

By now some of the other students had walked over to see the video. There were oohs and aahs, as at a display of fireworks. Indeed, it looked as though fireworks were going off on the edge of the moon's disk. But they weren't fireworks. They were erupting volcanoes.

The day of the sixth-grade science fair arrived. Each small group had prepared a presentation on a different moon of Jupiter or Saturn.

The reports on Europa and Ganymede focused on water and the remote possibility of life existing on them. The one on Callisto showed *Galileo*'s pictures of its surface, broken by millions of craters.

Touring the displays with Mr. Saenz was a short, red-haired woman who asked a lot of questions.

"All right, Group Io," Mr. Saenz said. "What can you tell us about the garden spot of the solar system?"

"Well," Linda began, "a lot of what we know about Io comes from the *Galileo* mission, of course. As we all know, *Galileo* was launched from the space shuttle in 1989 and has been taking pictures of Jupiter and its moons since 1995. It uses gravity to accelerate and change course, just like *Voyager* did."

Then Noah started running a video. It showed a simulation of *Galileo* appearing to accelerate past Jupiter and approach an orange-colored, metallic-looking moon.

"This is Io," said Noah, "the fifth moon of Jupiter and the third largest. It's the only body in the solar system besides Earth known to have active volcanoes. Boy, does it have volcanoes!"

Harcourt

Harcourt

TAKE-HOME BOOK
Times of Discovery
Use with "Cybersurfer."

THE VIRTUAL TUTOR

by Elaine Roche-Tombee
illustrated by Frank Carpenter

Harcourt

Award-Winning Assistance

Think of a time when you had trouble understanding something in school and a friend helped you. Make an award for that friend. On a separate sheet of paper, draw the award and tell why the friend deserves it.

Fold

School-Home Connection Listen as your child reads this book aloud. Then talk with your child about ways to get help if he or she is having trouble in school.

"Glad to know you're not going to fail math," Brian said.

"I was *never* going to *fail*," I retorted. "But it was nice to get help. Thanks, Piscator."

"Who are you talking to?" Devon teased.

"Oh, I think all three of you know," I said. "But the one who's been sending those messages is Fito. The reason I know that is because *piscator* means 'fisher,' and fishing is Fito's favorite hobby."

"Have another five-fifths of a slice," said Fito with a grin.

"This one's for you, Amalia!" said Mr. Baer. "I've got three-fourths of a pizza, and I divide it into six equal slices. What fraction of a pizza is each slice?"

"Uh. . . ." I was in a panic. I started to draw a pizza and slice it with my pencil, but it quickly became a jumble of crossing lines. Frantically I worked out the numbers. Three-fourths divided by six. . . ."

"Four and a half?" I said.

"Four and a half of a pizza?" said Mr. Baer.

I was bombarded with giggles from the class.

"Brian, what answer do you get?" said the teacher.

Harcourt

"That was embarrassing," I told my friends after school. We were at Leone's—eating a real pizza—Devon, Fito, Brian, and I. "I mean, dividing up three-fourths of a pizza and coming up with four and a half slices?"

"Maybe you need a tutor," Devon said helpfully.

"No, I'm good at math," I said. I always had been, until division of fractions reared its ugly head.

"There's no shame in admitting you need help," said Fito as he cast an imaginary fishing line. Fito is of the opinion that any moment not spent fishing is a waste of time. Weird.

I also remembered my English skills. When you meet a new and strange word, there's a place you can go to get better acquainted. It didn't help me with my math, but it did clear up a mystery.

Mr. Baer gave us a test on Friday. I was sure I had gotten an A. After school I went to Leone's with Devon, Fito, and Brian again.

Harcourt

It went on like that all week. Each day, Piscator left a little interactive graphic transmission that made the math clear. By the end of the week, I was dividing fractions with confidence—even out loud in class.

"You're dividing eight and one-fourth by one and a half," I explained. "Eight and one-fourth is thirty-three fourths. One and a half is three halves. You multiply by the reciprocal, which is two-thirds. . . ."

"I *don't* need help," I said, too loudly. "I made a mistake, that's all. Listen, could we not talk about math any more?"

"Sure," said Brian, wolfing down his last bite of pizza. "I'm late for my saxophone lesson anyway."

"And I've got to get over to the ice-skating rink," Devon said. She threw a few dollars down and flung her skates over her shoulder. "See you tomorrow, guys."

I did need help. I just didn't want a barrage of it from all sides. I felt bombarded with good intentions and still very confused.

There had to be some simple clue that would help me connect division of fractions to the real world. If pizza wouldn't do it, then what would?

That evening, after struggling with my math homework, I went online. A short break while I checked my messages was just what I needed.

I had a few online pen pals. I didn't know many of their real names, and we would probably never meet. We all went by screen names. I love music, so I use the name "noteworthy." Get it?

That evening I turned on my modem again to see if there was any help out there for me. Piscator had sent another transmission. This one was posted on the school's Web site.

"You have to write mixed numbers as fractions. Then you have to figure out which fraction is the divisor. You've got LESS than the amount of sugar you need for one recipe. How can your answer turn out to be MORE than one recipe?"

The problem was explained using pizza icons. I guess Piscator hadn't wanted to redo the graphics. I had no trouble seeing how you would divide two-thirds of a pizza among one and a third people. Maybe it was because I was feeling I had about one-third of a brain.

Harcourt

Harcourt

"You've got a cookie recipe that calls for one and a third cups of sugar," Mr. Baer said. "You have only two-thirds of a cup of sugar. What fraction of the recipe can you make?"

"Why can't you go to the store and buy more sugar?" That was Tim, the class clown.

"The stores are closed," said Mr. Baer. "Amalia?"

I knew you had to convert the mixed number to thirds and divide, but what did you divide by what?

"Two?" I answered.

"Two what?"

"Two cups of sugar?"

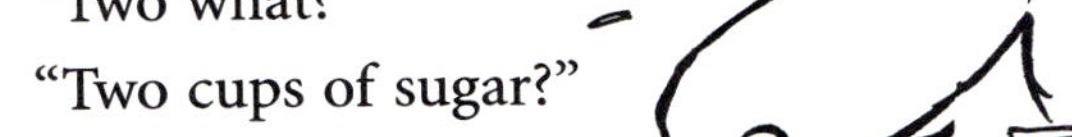

The modem hissed and whistled. The icons flashed. I had e-mail.

The message was not signed, but there was a return e-mail address: piscator@cnet.com.

There was an attached file. Normally, you don't open attachments from strangers. Some joker could trash your files with a virus. There has been quite a barrage of viruses in recent years. But piscator@cnet.com was no stranger. It was Devon, Fito, or Brian.

The attachment was a neat little interactive pizza graphic that made the problem perfectly clear. Someone had gone to a lot of trouble to help me.

Any of them could have done it. They were all in the computer club. Devon had designed the school's Web site. Fito was always making up computer games, most of which involved fishing. And Brian—well, when the computer in the school office crashed, Brian had brought it back online.

At school the next day, none of them would admit to sending the message. They all pretended they didn't know what I was talking about.

In math I bombed again.
This time we had to divide *by* fractions.

Harcourt

Harcourt

TAKE-HOME BOOK
Times of Discovery
Use with "The Fun They Had."

The Future of Reading

by **Frank Maltesi**
illustrated by J. Clay

Harcourt

Draw the Future

How do you think you will be living in the year 2025? On a separate sheet of paper, draw a picture that shows something of the world as it might be then.

School-Home Connection Listen as your child reads this book aloud. Then talk about ways technology has changed since you were in the sixth grade.

Fold

Harcourt

We'll still be reading books, though—just as we're still writing by hand, talking, and communicating without words. We'll just have this new way of recording and passing on information too.

What will it be? Thanks, but I'll let someone else predict the future. I'll only predict that whoever tries to predict it will be laughed at fifty years down the road.

Because the future isn't just unknown. It's really unimaginable.

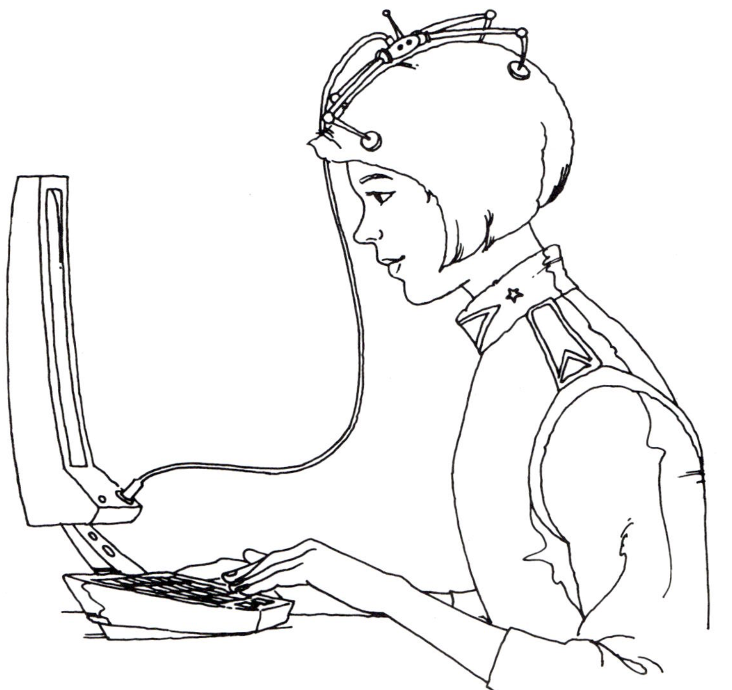

12

Fold

My friend Phil brought over his newest gadget the other day. It was an electronic book. It looked like a fine old book, bound in leather. It even opened like a book, once I found the "on" switch.

"You're holding the book of the future," Phil said loftily. "It doesn't waste trees, and it takes up very little space. You plug it into your computer and download a title from the Internet. When you've finished reading, you can download another one."

1

Harcourt

The screen showed an old favorite—*The Adventures of Tom Sawyer*, by Mark Twain. I leafed through a few pages. Well, actually, I pressed a button, and pages appeared on the screen. When I closed the book and opened it again, it automatically started where I had left off. There was a search function, too. It helped me find my favorite places quickly.

I handed the electronic book back to Phil. "Neat," I said. "But the type is hard to read, and it can't be adjusted like a TV set. It's expensive, too."

I think it will be the same with electronic books. Someone went to some trouble to make Phil's gadget look like a book. An early printer would recognize it easily—though he'd think the type was pretty ugly.

But the Internet isn't like a book. A book takes you from point to point. The Internet is more like a maze with many paths. When people really figure out how to make electronic books right, they won't be books at all. They will be something we can't imagine yet.

Harcourt

Here's an interesting fact about early printed books. Readers were used to handwritten books. So printers designed type to look like handwritten letters. It wasn't until printing had been around for a while that they decided to make many other styles of letters.

"The type will get better," he said nonchalantly, "and the price will come down. It always does with electronics."

Well, that much is true, so I let it go at that. I didn't want to get into a dispute with Phil by being scornful of his toy. But you can forget about that gadget being the book of the future.

If you want a good laugh, go to your public library. Go to the room where old magazines are kept. Ask the librarian to help you find articles from twenty or fifty years ago about what life would be like in the year 2000.

Harcourt

In 1950 you'd have seen pictures of colonies on the moon and cars that looked like spaceships. Robot maids were shown cleaning the house, and home telephones were equipped with two-way video.

Even science fiction was behind what was really happening. One popular novel of the 1950s was set in the twenty-fifth century. It had people moving from place to place by thought, but there were no computers. People in the story used manual typewriters.

For the first 4,500 years of writing, books were written by hand. That made them expensive. Only a few people could afford books. Few people knew how to read, so few people knew about the ideas books contained.

Then people figured out how to print using movable type. This invention adjusted attitudes in a hurry. Books could now be made cheaply, by the thousands. It became reasonable for more people to learn to read.

Of course, people never stopped writing by hand.

Harcourt

With the written word, you didn't have to be next to someone to share information. You could write a letter or a book, and people could read it even after you were dead. You could write loftily and move people to great deeds. You could write sorrowfully and move them to tears. You could even write something scornful if you felt the need.

In ancient times, writing was not done nonchalantly, as it often is today. Without computers, pencils, or ballpoint pens, writing was a much more difficult task.

Did writing turn talking and remembering into "things of the past"? We've been writing and reading for more than 5,000 years, and our voices and memories are still pretty useful.

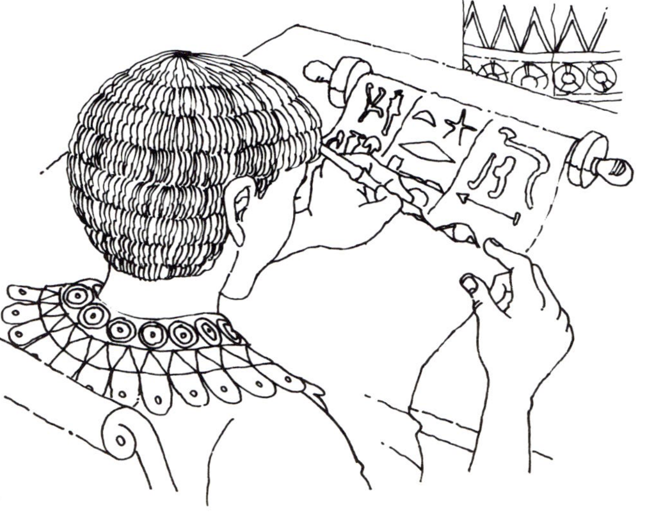

In 1980 people predicted that gasoline-powered cars were on their way out. Cars of 2000, they told us, would be powered by solar energy or hydrogen. Kitchens would be under computer control. In school, books and even teachers would largely be replaced by computers. But there wasn't a word about a network like the Internet.

Phil was in the sixth grade then. I wonder if he sorrowfully said good-bye to his teacher, thinking she was about to lose her job to a software package.

You can get a truer idea of the future of books by looking at the past. We human beings are always inventing new ways to record and pass on information. But we don't give up the old ways.

Early humans—we don't know exactly how early—developed speech. That gave them a great advantage over animals. But they kept on communicating without words, too. We still do today.

Harcourt

For thousands of years, the only way to record words was to remember them. People memorized lists of family names. They memorized long poems about heroes. They memorized other things too, such as who owed what to the king. But the information died with the person who remembered it, unless it was passed on by telling it to someone else.

Then writing was invented. This made a huge difference. People no longer had to remember everything. They could write things down and read them later. There could be no dispute about what people owed the king. He had it in writing.